Cyber Bullying

Cyber Bullying

A Prevention Curriculum for Grades 6–12

Susan P. Limber, Ph.D.
Robin M. Kowalski, Ph.D.
Patricia W. Agatston, Ph.D.

HAZELDEN

Hazelden
Center City, MN 55012
hazelden.org

© 2008 by Hazelden Foundation, all language versions worldwide
All rights reserved. Published 2008
Printed in the United States of America

No part of this publication may be reproduced, stored in a retrieval system, or transmitted in any form or by any means—electronic, mechanical, photocopying, recording, scanning, or otherwise—without the express written permission of the publisher. Failure to comply with these terms may expose you to legal action and damages for copyright infringement.

ISBN: 978-1-59285-596-4

The names, details, and circumstances may have been changed to protect the privacy of those mentioned in this publication.

Xanga Terms of Use, Member Conduct used with permission.

Design and production by David Farr, ImageSmythe

Interior illustrations by Chris Dyrud

Endorsements

"There is a critical need for quality instructional materials for students that address the new concern of cyber bullying. The professional background and excellent insight of Dr. Patricia W. Agatston, Dr. Robin M. Kowalski, and Dr. Susan P. Limber make this curriculum a very valuable contribution to the effort to effectively prevent and defuse the damage caused by hurtful online communications."

—Nancy Willard, M.S., J.D., author of
Cyberbullying and Cyberthreats: Responding to the Challenge of Online Social Aggression, Threats, and Distress
and executive director of the Center for Safe and Responsible Internet Use

"In *Cyber Bullying: A Prevention Curriculum for Grades 6–12*, Dr. Patricia W. Agatston, Dr. Robin M. Kowalski, and Dr. Susan P. Limber have created a resource as cutting edge as it is timeless. Their user-friendly curriculum—firmly grounded in both contemporary realities and traditional values—is a must for every institution faced with the task of educating the first generation of digital natives."

—Sharon Duke Estroff, author of
Can I Have a Cell Phone for Hanukkah?: The Essential Scoop on Raising Modern Jewish Kids

"I feel this curriculum will be a great benefit to schools and their students. Cyber bullying affects students on a daily basis, and this curriculum does a wonderful job of highlighting the changes that need to be made!"

—Tina Meier, The Megan Meier Foundation,
www.meganmeierfoundation.org

Contents

Acknowledgments   ix

How to Access the Resources on the CD-ROM   xi

Introductory Materials

Introduction to the Curriculum   1

Introduction to Cyber Bullying   11

Curriculum Scope and Sequence   19

Related National Academic Standards   21

Session Description and Preparation   25

Cyber Bullying Pre-Test/Post-Test   31

The Sessions

Session 1: What Is Bullying?   37

Session 2: What Is Cyber Bullying?   55

Session 3: How Does Cyber Bullying Affect People?   67

Session 4: Why Do People Cyber Bully Others?   81

Session 5: How Should You React to Cyber Bullying?   93

Session 6: Creating a Positive Cyber Site, Part I   105

Session 7: Creating a Positive Cyber Site, Part II   117

Session 8: Creating a Positive Cyber Site, Part III   123

Additional Materials

Teacher Training Preparation   129

Teacher Training Outline   133

Additional Resources   139

References   143

About the Authors   145

Acknowledgments

We would like to thank Alyse Cooper-Pribish of the Lovett School, Stephanie Meyer of Kennesaw Mountain High School, Jennie Brown and Jason Christy of Cayuse Prairie School, and Harriet Zimmer of the Balmoral Hill School, who along with their students provided invaluable feedback and suggestions for our curriculum. We also are indebted to Marlene Snyder, Ph.D., for her extremely helpful comments on an earlier draft. The editorial team of Pamela Foster, Bonnie Dudovitz, and Sue Thomas at Hazelden Publishing helped shepherd the development of this curriculum. Without their support, creativity, and assistance, this project would not have been produced. Finally, we thank our families—Andrew, Austin, Jack, Noah, Jordan, and Mary—who continue to inspire and support our work.

How to Access the Resources on the CD-ROM

The accompanying CD-ROM contains print resources, including electronic versions of the curriculum's handouts and templates and a number of related research information. All of these resources are in PDF format and can be accessed using Adobe Reader.® If you do not have Adobe Reader,® you can download it for free at www.adobe.com.

Whenever you see this icon in this guide, this means the needed resource is located on the CD-ROM. Notation that follows this icon indicates the document number for that resource's file. The first letter or letter/number pair indicates which folder the file is located in on the CD-ROM. The CD-ROM file numbers will help you easily locate and print the resource you are looking for. This symbol (SP) indicates the document is also available in Spanish.

To access these print resources, put the disk in your computer's CD-ROM player. Open your version of Adobe Reader.® Then open the documents by finding them on your CD-ROM drive. These resources cannot be modified, but they may be printed for use without concern for copyright infringement. For a list of what is contained on the CD-ROM, see the Read Me First document on the CD-ROM.

Introduction to the Curriculum

What Is *Cyber Bullying: A Prevention Curriculum for Grades 6–12*?

Cyber Bullying: A Prevention Curriculum for Grades 6–12 is a program that deals with attitudes and behaviors associated with cyber bullying. It consists of an eight-session curriculum, with these additional resources on a CD-ROM:

- reproducible parent resources
- program posters and student handouts
- resources to address cyber bullying schoolwide (tips for establishing a school policy, addressing legal concerns, etc.)
- peer leader training materials
- a training presentation on cyber bullying for program facilitators

Most materials needed to implement the program are included in this manual and CD-ROM. In addition, a Web site has been established that will provide up-to-date information about cyber bullying. This Web site can be accessed at www.hazelden.org/cyberbullying.

What Are the Program's Goals?

This program strives to achieve these goals:

- to raise students' and parents' awareness of what cyber bullying is and why it is so harmful
- to equip students with the skills and resources to treat each other respectfully when using cyber technologies

- to give students information about how to get help if they or others they know are being cyber bullied

- to equip students with the skills to use cyber technologies in positive ways

For more information on the learner outcomes for each session, turn to the Curriculum Scope and Sequence, page 19.

What Are the Components of *Cyber Bullying: A Prevention Curriculum for Grades 6–12*?

Eight-Session Curriculum

Each session can be completed in 50 minutes. The curriculum can be presented over a period of days or weeks, depending on your program's schedule. Each session includes detailed instructions on presenting the information, activities to reinforce the key concepts, and reproducible student handouts.

If you don't have time to present all eight sessions, consider condensing the curriculum into five sessions by omitting session 1 and combining sessions 6–8, with much of the project work in these sessions being completed as homework assignments.

Throughout the curriculum, some activities will be designated for middle school students or high school students. These include small-group discussion situations and a few other activities. These will be marked with the following icons: **Grade 6–8** **Grade 9–12**

The first five sessions of *Cyber Bullying* for students in middle school include journal entries from four fictional students who are learning about cyber bullying. Students will read the journal entries and discuss them in peer-led small groups. These journal entries engage students in the topic of the session and help them understand how to react to cyber bullying situations. The use of these fictional peers has been shown to be an effective teaching tool in evidence-based programs, such as Hazelden's Project Northland alcohol-use prevention curricula. It is important that you read through all the journal entries before beginning the program in your classroom so that you are aware of the story line and the characters' personalities.

The first five sessions of *Cyber Bullying* for students in high school include real-life stories—one per session. These real-life stories are based on actual events found in the news; however, names and some minor details have been changed and the characters' points of view dramatized. These real-life stories will make cyber bullying real to students and include questions to help spark discussion.

 An idea for presenting both the journal entries and the real-life stories would be to post these online in a blog or discussion board. If you do this, be sure to make posting accessible to only you and your students. Should you choose to post this content online, additional homework questions have been included at the end of each session to allow the students to answer online and to encourage them to apply the situations to their own lives.

In sessions 6–7, students will work on a small-group project to create plans for their own social-networking Web sites. (Students will not actually design sites, just create plans for them.) They will need to meet specific criteria to ensure the Web sites are safe for the users and promote positive interactions among teens. Each small group will present its Web site plan to the class during session 8. You may wish to assign some of this project work as homework or devote more class time to the assignment.

This program also includes a *Cyber Bullying* Pre-Test/Post-Test on page 31 that can be used to assess your students' knowledge and attitudes before and after you present the curriculum.

The curriculum uses peer leaders to lead a significant portion of each lesson, with the last three sessions serving as a cooperative-learning and project-based opportunity. Information about selecting and training peer leaders is found in I-10 the Peer Leader Packet on the CD-ROM. Peer leadership is a key component of this program and should not be omitted.

It is highly recommended that educators implement this program as part of an ongoing, comprehensive bullying prevention effort, such as the *Olweus Bullying Prevention Program (OBPP)*. More information on linking this curriculum to
I-9 *OBPP* is provided on the CD-ROM.

The Curriculum Scope and Sequence for the eight sessions is provided on page 19.

 I-11 You will find a Glossary of Cyber Terms for your reference on the CD-ROM. You may also wish to send this home for students' parents or guardians.

Parent/Guardian Materials

As in every strong prevention effort, it's important to actively involve your students' parents or guardians when implementing this program. A letter that informs parents and guardians about *Cyber Bullying: A Prevention Curriculum for Grades 6–12* is on the CD-ROM. It is recommended that this letter be sent to parents or guardians with the Glossary of Cyber Terms, also found on the CD-ROM, prior to implementing the program.

Each of the first five sessions also has a take-home assignment that students should do with a parent or guardian. After completing the assignment, adults and students are to sign the assignment and return it. If students are not able to have active parent or guardian participation, they can complete the activity with another close adult, such as a relative or neighbor, or if possible, a school staff person, such as a school counselor, may take part in this role.

All parent/guardian materials are provided in both English and Spanish.

Teacher Training Outline

You may want to multiply your efforts by training others to use *Cyber Bullying*. Preparation information and an outline for a 3-hour teacher training session are provided on pages 129–138. Consider hosting a training session for your school's faculty.

Teacher Training Presentation

Included on the CD-ROM is a training presentation that includes in-depth information and statistics on cyber bullying for teachers. This presentation, in a PDF file, can be used either as a self-led training or as part of the Teacher Training Outline.

Who Is the Intended Audience?

Cyber Bullying: A Prevention Curriculum for Grades 6–12 is designed for middle and high school students. This program would fit well within a health education, communications, technology, or general life skills curriculum (see Related National

Academic Standards, page 21). Teachers may use their discretion to adapt some activities to the ages and maturity levels of their students.

This curriculum involves trained student peer leaders who assist in teaching portions of the sessions. These leaders should be selected by their peers, two weeks prior to starting this curriculum. Encourage students to select fellow students whom they admire and respect. You will find more guidance on the peer leader selection process in Peer Leader Packet on the CD-ROM. You may also want to consider having older teens teach the program to younger teens. I-10

A school counselor could offer *Cyber Bullying* as part of a support group or counseling or education program, or it could be used in after-school, community, youth-enrichment (such as YMCA or Scouts), or faith-based youth programs.

Is This a Research-Based Program?

Cyber Bullying is not a research-based program, but it is based on the latest research in prevention and the topic of cyber bullying. Many of the session activities are patterned after prevention models that research has shown to be effective in decreasing negative student behaviors and increasing student attitudes toward refraining from negative behaviors.

These strategies include selecting and using peer leaders, providing parent/guardian-student activities, doing cooperative learning and project activities, and identifying the causes for the reasons students behave as they do.

The curriculum also recommends that schoolwide policies and procedures be established that can effectively address the issue of cyber bullying in a broad way, while establishing a climate conducive to positive interactions among students. Research-based programs, such as the *Olweus Bullying Prevention Program*, have proven that schoolwide efforts are more effective in addressing bullying than classroom components alone.

How Can We Address Cyber Bullying on a Schoolwide Level?

The *Cyber Bullying* curriculum should be taught within a school or organizational environment that supports the prevention of all forms of bullying, including cyber bullying, and does not tolerate its existence.

Here are some ways schools and community organizations can promote and support the message that cyber bullying is not tolerated:

1. Work to create a school environment in which respect and responsibility are promoted and bullying is not.

2. In conjunction with this classroom curriculum, implement a schoolwide program, such as the *Olweus Bullying Prevention Program*, to address bullying of all kinds.

3. Set clear school policies about reporting and addressing cyber bullying, whether it occurs on campus or not. (See the CD-ROM for information about creating school policies.)

4. Train staff to be aware of cyber bullying and to intervene appropriately. A training outline is provided on pages 133–138, and a training presentation is located on the CD-ROM. Have as many staff as possible complete this training.

5. If a student, parent, or guardian reports an incident of cyber bullying, take the situation seriously and proactively address the issue, even if the cyber bullying messages did not originate at your school.

6. Establish a no-use policy for cell phones on school grounds, if you don't have one already.

7. Teach the *Cyber Bullying* program to all students. Make program participation mandatory.

8. Host a cyber bullying prevention campaign. Involve students in making posters, announcements, and other promotional events on this important issue. You may also want to use the posters included on the CD-ROM.

9. Make young people aware of the resources in your school and in your community that are available to help them if they experience cyber bullying. Invite community representatives, such as law-enforcement officers, to speak to students about this issue.

10. Involve parents and guardians by hosting education programs for them and sending home the introductory parent/guardian letter and the

parent/guardian-student homework assignments provided with each lesson in this curriculum.

11. Establish procedures that parents and guardians can follow in reporting cyber bullying incidents to school staff. Make sure parents or guardians and staff know what these procedures are, and be sure to proactively address any cyber bullying incidents.

What Resources Are Available Online or in My Community to Help with This Topic?

You don't need to be an expert on cyber bullying to teach this curriculum. However, you may want to turn to community resources for help in presenting this issue or to learn more about it.

Most local law-enforcement agencies can provide guidance on how to address crimes related to cyber bullying. They may also be able to give guidance on how to track the source of anonymous cyber bullying messages.

Also check with local telecommunications companies to see whether they have any written materials on cyber technologies that will help you get up to speed on the types of technologies young people are using today.

Pages 139–142 of this curriculum provide a listing of additional resources available to you and for parents as you teach this curriculum.

What Should I Be Aware of When Teaching *Cyber Bullying: A Prevention Curriculum for Grades 6–12*?

Here are some helpful tips for teaching this curriculum:

1. During the first session, it's important to create a sense of trust and safety in your group. Be sure to discuss the need for ground rules (as outlined in session 1). Make sure students abide by these rules throughout the program.

2. When in a group setting, make sure students do not use real names or too many details when describing cyber bullying situations that they or

others have experienced. Encourage them to share any specific concerns they may have with you in private.

3. Be aware that some students in your class may be experiencing bullying, or cyber bullying in particular. Don't force students to answer questions or talk about their experiences if they're uncomfortable doing so.

4. Be aware that some students in your class may be bullying others.

5. It's difficult in a class environment to guarantee complete confidentiality. Warn students of this fact, so they don't reveal more than they are comfortable with. Also warn students ahead of time that if they reveal information about someone being hurt by others or someone who is considering hurting himself or herself, you are required to report this information.

6. Maintain respect during discussions. Allow people to offer opposing views, but to do so respectfully.

7. Peer leaders are a key component of this curriculum. As much as possible, allow students to select the peer leaders. If they choose someone who is known to be bullying others or is a negative peer leader, you may want to override their selection. On the other hand, the experience of leading others in bullying prevention efforts may have a strong influence on that student's behavior in the future. Supervision of all peer leaders is recommended to ensure they are not abusing their roles.

What Are Some Other Guidelines to Follow as I Teach *Cyber Bullying: A Prevention Curriculum for Grades 6–12*?

1. What if a student reveals she or he or a friend is being cyber bullied or bullied in other ways?

Before teaching this curriculum, check whether your school has a policy on reporting cyber bullying or bullying of any kind. If you are uncertain about reporting procedures, talk with your school leadership about how incidences should be reported.

While you are teaching this curriculum, a student may reveal that he or she is either being cyber bullied or is cyber bullying others. As previously noted, it's important at the outset of the program to let students know what you will do upon learning this information, so they don't feel set up or betrayed by the action you take.

If a student reveals information during a class discussion, do not continue discussing the issue with everyone present. Invite the student to talk privately with you afterward. Write down any information the student provides.

Don't try to solve this problem on your own. Consult with appropriate school officials and the student's parents or guardians.

2. *What should you do if, while visiting a social-networking Web site, you find examples of cyber bullying among your students?*

As you become more familiar with cyber technologies that students are using, you may find instances in which students in your school or district are engaged in cyber bullying or other worrisome behaviors on the Internet. Whenever possible, print the information and share it with your school leadership. In most cases, inappropriate information added to social-networking Web sites can be traced back to the person who created it. Depending on the seriousness of the issue, you may need to involve law-enforcement officials.

3. *What if parents or guardians are uncomfortable with the topic and don't want their children involved?*

On rare occasions, parents or guardians may express reservations about their child or children being taught this cyber bullying prevention curriculum. This may occur because some parents or guardians may not want their child or children using certain cyber technologies or may be concerned about Internet safety.

While participating in the cyber bullying prevention program, students will not be working online except where optionally suggested. Care has also been taken to make sure the program does not encourage cyber technology use or give students new ideas of how to cyber bully one another.

When parents or guardians raise concerns, encourage them to review the curriculum. Tell them about the prevalence of cyber bullying among teens and the importance of addressing this issue in a preventative way. Discuss any additional concerns they may have. If they still voice reservations, it may be best to have the students complete an alternate project on a related topic.

Be sure to let parents and guardians know about the curriculum in advance through school newsletters or informational meetings and by sending home a letter explaining the curriculum. You will find a sample letter on the CD-ROM.

Introduction to Cyber Bullying

Danielle was a new student at the middle school. It was hard making new friends and finding ways to fit in. For some reason, the popular girls in her class didn't like her. They called her names and told her not to sit anywhere near them in the cafeteria.

The bullying became even worse when these girls decided to create a page on a popular social-networking Web site where they posted unflattering pictures of Danielle and wrote terrible messages.

Danielle found out about it when she saw several girls secretly looking at a computer and laughing in the library. Danielle was shocked to see the Web site, but she didn't want to tell any adults because she feared the cyber bullying might get even worse.

For many students like Danielle, cyber bullying is a serious issue that affects their sense of well-being and their ability to learn in the classroom. To understand what cyber bullying is, it is important to first understand what bullying is.

What Is Bullying?

Dan Olweus, Ph.D., a pioneer researcher in the area of bullying, has defined bullying in this way:

> Bullying is when someone repeatedly and on purpose says or does mean or hurtful things to another person who has a hard time defending himself or herself (Olweus et al. 2007).

There are both direct and indirect forms of bullying. The more direct forms include physical actions, such as hitting someone, taking or damaging someone else's things, or saying mean or hurtful things to someone.

Indirect forms of bullying are more concealed and subtle, and it is more difficult to determine who is causing the bullying. Examples include social exclusion, spreading rumors, and cyber bullying.

Dr. Olweus's research determined that students play a variety of roles in bullying situations. These roles make up what he called the Bullying Circle. These roles are diagrammed below.

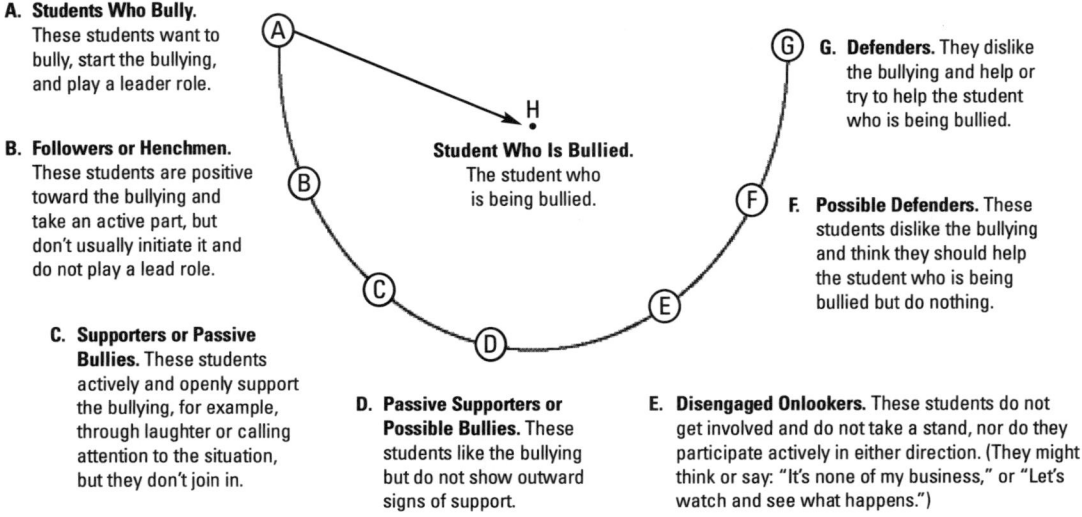

A. **Students Who Bully.** These students want to bully, start the bullying, and play a leader role.

B. **Followers or Henchmen.** These students are positive toward the bullying and take an active part, but don't usually initiate it and do not play a lead role.

C. **Supporters or Passive Bullies.** These students actively and openly support the bullying, for example, through laughter or calling attention to the situation, but they don't join in.

D. **Passive Supporters or Possible Bullies.** These students like the bullying but do not show outward signs of support.

E. **Disengaged Onlookers.** These students do not get involved and do not take a stand, nor do they participate actively in either direction. (They might think or say: "It's none of my business," or "Let's watch and see what happens.")

F. **Possible Defenders.** These students dislike the bullying and think they should help the student who is being bullied but do nothing.

G. **Defenders.** They dislike the bullying and help or try to help the student who is being bullied.

H. **Student Who Is Bullied.** The student who is being bullied.

In effective bullying prevention efforts, it is helpful to focus on changing the attitudes and behaviors of bystanders (positions C–F in the Bullying Circle above), who generally make up 80 percent of a school's student body. The goal is to move these bystanders into the positions of defending or helping the student who is being bullied. This is a primary goal of *Cyber Bullying: A Prevention Curriculum for Grades 6–12*.

What Is Cyber Bullying?

Cyber bullying is bullying through email, instant messaging (IMing), chat room exchanges, Web site posts, or digital messages or images sent to a cellular phone or personal digital assistant (PDA) (Kowalski et al. 2008). Cyber bullying, like traditional bullying, involves an imbalance of power and a negative action that is often repeated.

In traditional forms of bullying, individuals may have more power over another by being bigger, stronger, or more popular. With cyber bullying, an individual may have more power just by being able to instantly share negative comments or photographs with a multitude of people via email, instant messaging, text messaging, or Web site posts. Cyber bullying may also involve several individuals targeting one individual or a more popular student targeting a less popular classmate.

Traditional bullying is also defined by mean or negative actions being repeated and occurring over time. When someone is cyber bullied, this repetition of negative behavior can occur by sending one embarrassing photo or one degrading email message, which may in turn be forwarded to an entire class or grade level. The perpetrator, who is usually known in a traditional bullying situation, might go unidentified in the case of cyber bullying.

Traditional bullying usually occurs in a certain time and space, perhaps during school in the bathrooms or the hallways. Students who are bullied can usually find some relief at home or away from school. When a student is cyber bullied, the incident can happen whenever someone turns on their computer or goes online. This often happens at home at any time of the day or night.

Cyber bullying poses unique challenges because it frequently happens outside the school setting, and thus may be difficult for educators to observe. In addition, students may feel invisible or anonymous online, which may lead to a greater willingness to engage in negative actions. Finally, without face-to-face interaction, students who cyber bully have no opportunity to witness the emotional distress their comments or actions may be inflicting on a peer.

There is a bright spot, however. Although direct evidence may be hard to obtain in many traditional forms of bullying, cyber bullying typically involves a form of communication that can be saved and printed from a computer or saved on a cell phone. Such obvious evidence can be helpful when intervening in cyber bullying incidences.

Why Should Schools Address the Issue of Cyber Bullying?

Schools have rapidly embraced technology because of its ability to offer advanced learning opportunities and resources to students. Teachers use blogs, students post completed assignments online, and some schools issue laptops and PDAs to students as instructional tools. By embracing technology and encouraging students to explore its various forms, educators also have a duty to teach students to use such technologies in a responsible manner.

In addition, many schools are already adopting comprehensive bullying prevention programs, such as the *Olweus Bullying Prevention Program,* or are at least teaching classroom lessons that address bullying behaviors. Cyber bullying is one form of bullying that should be specifically addressed as part of these comprehensive efforts.

Research has shown that not all students perceive cyber bullying as a form of bullying behavior (Kowalski et al. 2008). For that reason, classroom lessons and discussions that focus directly on cyber bullying are critical to preventing it from flourishing.

How Prevalent Is Cyber Bullying?

Although the numbers vary based on the methods used to gather the data, the Pew Internet Survey found that almost one-third of teens had experienced cyber bullying (Lenhart 2007). In addition, Kowalski and Limber (2007) found that 22 percent of middle school students had some form of involvement in cyber bullying (defined as being cyber bullied or cyber bullying others at least once in the previous couple of months). Thus, high percentages of students are being affected by this behavior. Without specific prevention efforts, the numbers will likely increase as more students become "wired" at increasingly younger ages.

What Are the Warning Signs of Cyber Bullying?

The warning signs of cyber bullying are similar to those for traditional bullying in terms of emotional effects; however, there are some differences. For example, a bruise or torn clothing is not expected as a sign that a child is being cyber bullied, but it is also important to keep in mind that some children who are cyber bullied may also be experiencing traditional bullying at school.

A child may be experiencing cyber bullying if he or she

- appears sad, moody, or anxious.
- avoids school.
- withdraws from or shows a lack of interest in social activities.
- experiences a drop in grades or decline in academic performance.
- appears upset after using the computer or being online.
- appears upset after viewing a text message.

If a child shows any of these warning signs, it is important to talk with the child and investigate his or her online presence to determine whether cyber bullying is occurring and to offer help when needed.

How Does Cyber Bullying Affect Students, Schools, and Communities?

Current research demonstrates that students who are targets of traditional bullying are more likely to have low self-esteem (Olweus 1978; Rigby and Slee 1993), be anxious and depressed (Juvonen, Graham, and Schuster 2003), and experience a variety of health problems, such as stomachaches, headaches, fatigue, and difficulty sleeping and eating (Fekkes et al. 2004). They also are more likely to have thoughts of suicide (Rigby 1997). Students who are afraid to come to school and are being targeted by peer abuse, such as cyber bullying, are not likely to give their full attention to academics. Students who are bullied have higher absenteeism rates and lower grades than students who are not bullied (Arseneault et al. 2006; Eisenberg et al. 2003; Rigby 1997).

Research on cyber bullying specifically suggests that students involved in cyber bullying, particularly those who are cyber bullied and who also cyber bully others, are more likely to be anxious, depressed, and have low self-esteem than students who are not involved. Students who are cyber bullied are also more likely to have lower grades and higher absenteeism rates than those students not involved (Kowalski et al. 2008).

Although cyber bullying usually occurs outside of the school day, it can have an impact at school when students are afraid to face their peer group after receiving mean comments or messages at home. In addition, many students are targets of traditional bullying at school and cyber bullying at home, which can leave them feeling there is no safe haven available to them.

Educators and administrators frequently observe that investigating and intervening in cyber bullying incidents can be very time-consuming. Parents and guardians also report feeling victimized when their children are targeted by cyber bullying (Kowalski et al. 2008). Just as schools discuss character education for the real world, they need to discuss how students treat one another in the online world as technology advances.

What Should Teachers Do If They Know or Suspect Cyber Bullying Is Occurring?

It is important to educate students about how to report all forms of bullying, including cyber bullying, to adults at school and at home. This should be part of a teacher's ongoing classroom discussions about bullying. Session 5 in this curriculum also teaches students these skills.

If a teacher suspects a student is being cyber bullied, the teacher should advise the student to save any evidence of the cyber bullying and report it by attaching a copy of the printed online communications as evidence. The student can bring the evidence to the teacher, a school counselor, or an administrator. If there is no evidence, the student should still report the cyber bullying and include a description of what is taking place, so a counselor or administrator can investigate and speak with the parties involved.

Although all adults at school should have an understanding of cyber bullying and should be open to receiving reports of cyber bullying, it will be most helpful to identify individuals at each school who are particularly knowledgeable about bullying and cyber bullying. These individuals will want to investigate and determine whether any on-campus traditional bullying and/or cyber bullying is occurring with off-campus cyber bullying. Check with your school administrators to determine the appropriate person to whom cyber bullying incidences should be reported.

Any evidence of bullying at school should be addressed with consistent consequences for the student engaged in bullying behavior and with heightened adult supervision around the targeted student. In addition, positive bystanders should be encouraged to support the targeted student through a variety of means, such as those suggested in this curriculum.

Some forms of cyber bullying are illegal. Educators should always contact law-enforcement officials if communications involve death threats, extortion, intimidation, or threats based on race, religion, gender, or sexual orientation, or if there is any evidence of sexual exploitation (Kowalski et al. 2008; Willard 2007). (See the CD-ROM's files on state laws, litigation, and guidelines for administrators for additional guidance about legal issues and cyber bullying.)

I-1 through 1-3

If the cyber bullying takes place off campus, does not potentially violate the law, and is not accompanied by on-campus bullying, educators may be somewhat more limited in actions they can take (for example, sanctions may violate a student's First Amendment rights). But they can still take steps to intervene by conferring separately with the students involved and their parents or guardians. Teachers can try to monitor any interactions between the involved students more closely or perhaps change class schedules to minimize the contact between the students. They can advise the student who is targeted to save the evidence in case the situation escalates. School counselors might also get involved by arranging a meeting between the students to resolve the situation, although care must be taken in doing so. Educators can also assist the parents or guardians of a targeted student by providing educational literature about preventing and responding to cyber bullying and how to report offensive profiles to social-networking Web sites. This educational literature is provided on the curriculum CD-ROM.

I-5
I-6
I-13

Curriculum Scope and Sequence

Session 1: What Is Bullying?	Session 2: What Is Cyber Bullying?	Session 3: How Does Cyber Bullying Affect People?	Session 4: Why Do People Cyber Bully Others?
By the end of this session, students will be able to do the following:			
• define bullying • identify examples of bullying • identify the roles students play in the Bullying Circle • identify rules against bullying	• define cyber bullying • identify the technologies used in cyber bullying • identify cyber bullying situations	• identify the effects of cyber bullying on the student who is bullied, the bystanders, and the student(s) who bully • identify how to use technology in a positive way	• identify reasons people think they can cyber bully others • state why they think cyber bullying is unacceptable

Session 5: How Should You React to Cyber Bullying?	Session 6: Creating a Positive Cyber Site, Part I	Session 7: Creating a Positive Cyber Site, Part II	Session 8: Creating a Positive Cyber Site, Part III
By the end of this session, students will be able to do the following:			
• identify what steps to take if they are cyber bullied • identify what steps to take if they know someone else is being cyber bullied	• describe how some social-networking Web sites began • explain what social-networking Web sites do to curb abuse • describe the steps in planning a social-networking Web site • describe rules for belonging to some social-networking Web sites	• describe the components of an effective presentation • identify how they personally will commit themselves to stop or prevent cyber bullying	• make a public commitment to prevent cyber bullying • identify positive ways to use social-networking Web sites

Related National Academic Standards

Using *Cyber Bullying: A Prevention Curriculum for Grades 6–12* will help you meet the following national academic standards:

Health Education Standards*

Students in grades 6–8 will

- describe how peers influence healthy and unhealthy behaviors.

- analyze how the school and community can affect personal health practices and behaviors.

- analyze how messages from media influence health behaviors.

- analyze the influence of technology on personal and family health.

- apply effective verbal and nonverbal communication skills to enhance health.

- demonstrate how to ask for assistance to enhance the health of self and others.

- demonstrate behaviors that avoid or reduce health risks to self and others.

- work cooperatively to advocate for healthy individuals, families, and schools.

- identify ways in which health messages and communication techniques can be altered for different audiences.

---

*Joint Committee on National Health Education Standards. *National Health Education Standards, Second Edition, Achieving Excellence.* The American Cancer Society. 2007.

Students in grades 9–12 will

- analyze how peers influence healthy and unhealthy behaviors.

- evaluate how the school and community can affect personal health practices and behaviors.

- evaluate the effect of media on personal and family health.

- evaluate the impact of technology on personal, family, and community health.

- use skills for communicating effectively with family, peers, and others to enhance health.

- demonstrate how to ask for and offer assistance to enhance the health of self and others.

- demonstrate a variety of behaviors that avoid or reduce health risks to self and others.

- work cooperatively as an advocate for improving personal, family, and community health.

- adapt health messages and communication techniques to a specific target audience.

Technology Education Standards*

Communication and Collaboration

Students in grades 6–12 will

- interact, collaborate, and publish with peers, experts, or others, employing a variety of digital environments and media.

- communicate information and ideas effectively to multiple audiences using a variety of media and formats.

- contribute to project teams to produce original works or solve problems.

---

*National Educational Technology Standards for Students, Second Edition, © 2007, ISTE® (International Society for Technology in Education), www.iste.org. All rights reserved.

Critical Thinking, Problem-Solving, and Decision-Making

Students in grades 6–12 will

- identify and define authentic problems and significant questions for investigation.

- plan and manage activities to develop a solution or complete a project.

- collect and analyze data to identify solutions and make informed decisions.

- use multiple processes and diverse perspectives to explore alternate solutions.

Digital Citizenship

Students in grades 6–12 will

- advocate and practice safe, legal, and responsible use of information and technology.

- exhibit a positive attitude toward using technology that supports collaboration, learning, and productivity.

- demonstrate personal responsibility for lifelong learning.

- exhibit leadership for digital citizenship.

Session Description and Preparation

Here is an overview of the preparation you'll need to do to teach each *Cyber Bullying* session.

Session Title	Session Description	Materials Needed	Preparation Needed
Session 1: What Is Bullying?	Through student journal entries or a real-life story, small- and large-group discussions, and word collages, students will define bullying and learn about the Bullying Circle diagram and the rules against bullying.	• CD-ROM materials • Parent/Guardian Letter I-12 (SP) • Completed Why Should We Talk About Cyber Bullying? peer leader handouts I-10 • Grade 6–8 Session 1 Journal Entries S1-1 • Grade 9–12 Session 1 Real-Life Story S1-2 • Bullying Circle diagram S1-3 • The Four Anti-Bullying Rules sheet S1-4 • Homework Assignment 1 S1-5 (SP) • *Optional:* Overhead or LCD projector, dry-erase board, or chalkboard • *Optional:* Two transparency sheets • Collage materials	• Print and send the Parent/Guardian Letter home with each student prior to starting the program. • Grade 6–8 Copy the Session 1 Journal Entries. • Grade 9–12 Copy the Session 1 Real-Life Story. • Gather the collage materials. • Copy Homework Assignment 1. • Read through all the journal entries for sessions 1–6. • Return the Why Should We Talk About Cyber Bullying? handouts to their peer leader authors. • *Optional:* Photocopy the Bullying Circle diagram and the Four Anti-Bullying Rules sheet onto transparency sheets.

■ Cyber Bullying

Session Title	Session Description	Materials Needed	Preparation Needed

Session 2: What Is Cyber Bullying?	Through student journal entries or a real-life story, small- and large-group discussions, and a board game, students will understand what cyber bullying is and is not, and the technologies used to cyber bully.	• CD-ROM materials
		  • **Grade 6–8** Session 2 Journal Entries S2-1
		  • **Grade 9–12** Session 2 Real-Life Story S2-2
		  • Is It or Isn't It? game board S2-4
		  • Is It or Isn't It? game cards S2-5
		  • Is It or Isn't It? Peer Leader Instructions S2-3
		  • Homework Assignment 2 S2-6 (SP)
		• Scissors
		• Blank paper (or real game pawns)
		• Pens or pencils
		• Dice
		• *Optional:* Computer
			• **Grade 6–8** Copy the Session 2 Journal Entries.
			• **Grade 9–12** Copy the Session 2 Real-Life Story.
			• Copy the Is It or Isn't It? game board.
			• Copy and cut out the Is It or Isn't It? game cards.
			• Cut the blank paper into small game pieces, or use real game pawns.
			• Copy the Is It or Isn't It? Peer Leader Instructions.
			• Gather dice.
			• Copy Homework Assignment 2.

Session Description and Preparation

Session Title	Session Description	Materials Needed	Preparation Needed
Session 3: How Does Cyber Bullying Affect People?	Through student journal entries or a real-life story, and group discussion, students will understand the serious effects of cyber bullying. Students will also develop a positive text-message language to explore how to use technology in a positive way.	• CD-ROM materials • **Grade 6–8** Session 3 Journal Entries S3-1 • **Grade 9–12** Session 3 Real-Life Story S3-2 • Text Talk worksheets S3-3 • Homework Assignment 3 S3-4 (SP) • Magazines or newspapers • One sheet of poster board • Scissors • Glue	• **Grade 6–8** Copy the Session 3 Journal Entries. • **Grade 9–12** Copy the Session 3 Real-Life Story. • Copy the Text Talk worksheets. • Copy Homework Assignment 3. • Look through the magazines or newspaper to find and cut out pictures of the following: a person (could be a celebrity), a house, a school, a group of friends, a key, and someone laughing. Lightly glue the picture of the person in the middle of the poster board and glue the rest of the pictures around the person. Label each picture in this manner: • Person = Self-Esteem • Group of Friends = Friends • School = School/Learning • Laughing Person = Happiness • Key = Safety • House = Home/Family

■ Cyber Bullying

Session Title	Session Description	Materials Needed	Preparation Needed
Session 4: Why Do People Cyber Bully Others?	Through journal entries or a real-life story and small- and large-group discussions, students will understand why teens cyber bully others. Then through the creation of public service announcements (PSAs), students will take steps to prevent cyber bullying and take a stand against it.	• CD-ROM materials 　• [Grade 6–8] Session 4 Journal Entries S4-1 　• [Grade 9–12] Session 4 Real-Life Story S4-2 　• PSA Planning Sheet S4-3 　• Homework Assignment 4 S4-4 (SP) • Your school's bullying or cyber bullying policy, if available • Transparency and overhead projector, or a chalkboard and chalk • Materials for PSAs, such as poster board, video cameras, CD recorders	• [Grade 6–8] Copy the Session 4 Journal Entries. • [Grade 9–12] Copy the Session 4 Real-Life Story. • Copy the PSA Planning Sheet. • Copy Homework Assignment 4. • Before class, check with your school administrator about what policies are in place regarding cyber bullying and review the policies. If none are in place, maybe your class can lobby for some.

Session Title	Session Description	Materials Needed	Preparation Needed
Session 5: How Should You React to Cyber Bullying?	Through journal entries, a real-life story and small- and large-group discussions, and sample situations, students will learn what to do if someone cyber bullies them or another person.	• CD-ROM materials • **Grade 6–8** Session 5 Journal Entries S5-1 • **Grade 9–12** Session 5 Real-Life Story S5-2 • Do First poster and handout S5-3 • Question Cube S5-4 • What Would You Do If…? situation sheet S5-5 • Homework Assignment 5 S5-6 (SP) • Chalkboard and chalk, flipchart or poster board and markers • Your school's bullying or cyber bullying policy, if available • Scissors • Clear tape	• **Grade 6–8** Copy the Session 5 Journal Entries. • **Grade 9–12** Copy the Session 5 Real-Life Story. • Copy the Do First handout. • Print the Do First poster and display it in your space. • Copy, cut, and assemble the Question Cubes. • Select the situations for your classroom and print the What Would You Do If…? situation sheets. • Copy Homework Assignment 5.

Cyber Bullying

Session Title	Session Description	Materials Needed	Preparation Needed
Session 6: Creating a Positive Cyber Site, Part I	Through a small-group project, students will create plans for their own social-networking Web sites that will promote safe and positive Internet use.	• CD-ROM materials • Xanga Terms of Use, Member Conduct S6-2 • Web Site Planning Packet S6-3 • Facts of the Feature sheets S6-4 • *Grade 6-8* Session 6 Journal Entries S6-1 • Overhead projector and transparency paper, or computer and LCD projector.	• Print the Xanga information and make transparencies. Or prepare them on PowerPoint slides. • Copy the Web Site Planning Packet. • Copy the Facts of the Feature sheet. • *Grade 6-8* Copy the Session 6 Journal Entries. • Visit some social-networking Web sites so you are familiar with their format and content.
Session 7: Creating a Positive Cyber Site, Part II	Students will fill out a form to commit to helping stop cyber bullying and to explain what they will do if they are aware of cyber bullying situations. Students will continue to work on their small-group project.	• CD-ROM materials • Cyber Solutions sheet S7-1 • Materials for the project, including large paper or poster board, markers, and colored pencils • *Optional:* Computers	• Copy the Cyber Solutions sheet. • Gather project materials.
Session 8: Creating a Positive Cyber Site, Part III	Students will read one of their commitments to the class about how they will stop and/or prevent cyber bullying. They will also present their social-networking Web site project plans to the class.	• CD-ROM materials • Web Site Plan Presentation Score Sheet S8-1 • *Optional:* Video camera to film the presentations	• Copy the Web Site Plan Presentation Score Sheet. • *Optional:* Make sure the video camera is ready for filming.

Cyber Bullying Pre-Test/Post-Test

Name_____ Class Period_____

Write your answers in the spaces provided.

1. What is the definition of *bullying?*

   _____
   _____
   _____
   _____

2. List three roles people could play in the Bullying Circle.

   a. _____

   b. _____

   c. _____

3. List three technologies that can be used in cyber bullying.

   a. _____

   b. _____

■ Cyber Bullying

4. List two ways that cyber bullying differs from traditional bullying.

   a. _____

   b. _____

5. List two ways that being cyber bullied might affect someone your age.

   a. _____

   b. _____

6. List two reasons someone might cyber bully someone else.

   a. _____

   b. _____

7. List three things you could do if you were cyber bullied.

   a. _____

   b. _____

   c. _____

8. List three things that most social-networking Web sites don't allow.

   a. _____

   b. _____

   c. _____

Cyber Bullying *Pre-test/Post-test*

**Write "T" for True or "F" for False
on the line in front of each statement below.**

_____ 9. Only two people are involved in a bullying situation—the person who bullies and the person who is bullied.

_____ 10. Sending an embarrassing or insulting photo through email is cyber bullying.

_____ 11. Cyber bullying can only occur through the Internet.

_____ 12. Students who are cyber bullied often don't want to go to school.

_____ 13. Showing empathy means donating money to help those who are cyber bullied.

_____ 14. One reason people cyber bully others is because they think no one will find out who did it.

_____ 15. Everything that is done on a computer is recorded inside it.

_____ 16. It's important to save the evidence if you are cyber bullied.

_____ 17. A good way to deal with cyber bullying is to retaliate immediately.

_____ 18. Social-networking Web sites cannot take any action against someone who is using the site to abuse or insult others.

Answers for the Pre-Test/Post-Test

1. *Bullying* is when someone repeatedly and on purpose says or does mean or hurtful things to another person who has a hard time defending himself or herself.

2. Possible answers include descriptions of these eight participants:

    - person who is bullied

    - person who is bullying someone

    - followers of the person who is doing the bullying who join in after it starts

    - supporters of the person who is doing the bullying who don't join in but encourage or laugh at the bullying

    - passive supporters who like the bullying but don't show it

    - onlookers who don't have a positive or negative reaction

    - possible defenders who don't like the bullying and think they should do something about it but do nothing

    - defenders who try to help the person who is being bullied

3. Possible answers include these technologies:

    - cell phones/text messages

    - Internet/computer

    - Web sites

    - email

    - instant messaging

4. Possible answers include these differences:

    - Cyber bullying can reach and involve many people much more quickly than traditional bullying.

    - People who might not bully someone face to face might cyber bully someone because they can't be seen and think they are anonymous.

- Traditional bullying usually involves an imbalance of power. Students who bully target others they think won't fight back. Because people who cyber bully think they are anonymous, they might not be more physically or socially powerful but can feel more powerful by using technology.

- Traditional forms of bullying can cause physical harm and psychological harm. In most cases, cyber bullying causes psychological harm.

- Traditional bullying is usually limited to the people in the immediate area where the bullying is taking place. Cyber bullying can reach many people immediately—and often the target is unaware of who these people are.

- Traditional bullying usually has a time and place, such as the school playground at recess. Cyber bullying can happen anytime and any place. For a while, the target may even be unaware that it is happening.

- It is usually apparent who is doing traditional bullying. It is often difficult to find out who is doing cyber bullying.

5. Teens who are cyber bullied can become depressed, anxious, nervous, and fearful, and may have low self-esteem, avoid going to school, do poorly in school, lose friends, have damaged reputations, and feel unsafe.

6. People may cyber bully for these reasons:

    - They think they can be anonymous.

    - They can't be seen.

    - They don't have to see the other person's reactions.

    - Everybody does it, so it's no big deal.

    - They like making someone else feel bad.

7. Possible answers include ignore it, block the sender, tell an adult, respond but don't retaliate, trace the sender, contact the Internet service provider or social-networking Web site, and save the evidence.

8. Possible answers include these:

   - harmful, threatening, obscene, abusive, racist language
   - content that harms minors in some way
   - stalking behavior
   - content that provides instructions for or promotion of illegal activities
   - pornographic content of minors
   - impersonating another user or person
   - soliciting personal information for anyone under the age of eighteen
   - providing a false age or birthday

9. False
10. True
11. False
12. True
13. False
14. True
15. True
16. True
17. False
18. False

SESSION 1

What Is Bullying?

Description

Through student journal entries or a real-life story, small- and large-group discussions, and word collages, students will define bullying, and learn about the Bullying Circle and rules against bullying.

Learner Outcomes

By the end of this session, students will be able to

- define *bullying*.
- identify examples of bullying.
- identify the roles students play in the Bullying Circle.
- identify rules against bullying.

Materials Needed

☐ CD-ROM materials:

- Parent/Guardian Letter I-12 (SP)
- The completed Why Should We Talk About Cyber Bullying? peer leader handouts (completed during peer leader training) I-10

SESSION 1 AT A GLANCE

Total Time: 50 minutes

Part 1:
Program Introduction
(5 minutes)

Part 2:
Journal Entries/ Real-Life Story and Discussion
(20 minutes)

Part 3:
Creating Anti- Bullying Collages and Posters
(20 minutes)

Part 4:
Conclusion and Homework Assignment
(5 minutes)

■ Cyber Bullying

TEACHER TIP
Make sure you read all the journal entries for sessions 1–6 before beginning the program. It is important that you know the flow of the story and the sequence of material as it is presented.

- Session 1 Journal Entries S1-1
- Session 1 Real-Life Story S1-2
- Bullying Circle diagram S1-3
- The Four Anti-Bullying Rules sheet S1-4
- Homework Assignment 1 S1-5 (SP)

☐ Collage materials including the following:

- Poster board or large pieces of paper (one per small group of three to four students with one peer leader)
- Magazines
- Newspapers
- Scissors
- Glue or tape
- Markers and/or crayons
- Pens or pencils

☐ *Optional:* Overhead, or LCD projector, dry-erase board, or chalkboard

☐ *Optional:* Two transparency sheets

Preparation Needed

1. Print out and send the Parent/Guardian Letter home with each student prior to starting the program.

2. Print out the Session 1 Journal Entries, one set per student.

   Students will be working on the journal entries in their small groups. Each small group will work on a different characters and all students in that small group will need a copy of that character's journal entry. However, you

TEACHER TIP
This lesson includes a lot of material to cover. You may want to watch your time closely or divide this into two class periods.

may wish to give all students a copy of all four journal entries to follow along as they are read aloud. You may also want to have extra copies so that members of a small group could discuss a second character if they finish their work early.

3. Print out the Session 1 Real-Life Story, one copy per student.

4. Gather the collage materials.

5. Print out and make copies of Homework Assignment 1, one per student.

6. Read through all of the journal entries for sessions 1–6, so you will know how the stories progress as the program continues.

7. Return the Why Should We Talk About Cyber Bullying? handouts to their peer leader authors.

8. If you are using the overhead projector, photocopy the Bullying Circle diagram and the Four Anti-Bullying Rules sheet onto transparency sheets. If you are using an LCD projector, make sure you have these documents ready to go on your computer. If you are using a dry-erase board or chalkboard, write these out for the students to see.

SESSION OUTLINE

PART 1
5 minutes

▶ **Program Introduction**

The purpose of part 1 is to introduce the *Cyber Bullying* curriculum to students and to get them thinking about why it is important to discuss the topic of bullying. The role of peer leaders will also be explained to the students.

1. Explain to the students:

   Today we are starting a program about cyber bullying. How many of you have heard this term before? Some of you may already have or know someone who has experienced cyber bullying, while some of you may not know what it is. Over the next eight sessions, we will learn more about cyber bullying and what we can do to prevent it.

   One exciting thing about this program is that the students you chose to be peer leaders will be leading much of the time during our sessions.

2. Introduce the peer leaders by having them stand. Call on each one to read his or her Why Should We Talk About Cyber Bullying? statement.

3. Thank the peer leaders and ask the rest of the class:

   Why do you think it is important for us to talk about cyber bullying? Why is it important even if it hasn't happened to you and you haven't cyber bullied anyone?

   Allow time for students to respond between questions.

4. Summarize by saying:

Cyber bullying affects everyone, even if you haven't experienced it. You may be a part of cyber bullying even if you don't know it. For example, if you've forwarded an email that makes fun of someone to one or more friends, that is considered cyber bullying.

To understand what cyber bullying is, it helps to first learn more about what bullying is and how we can prevent it. This is what we will be talking about today.

■ Cyber Bullying

PART 2
20 minutes

▶ **Journal Entries/Real-Life Story and Discussion**

The purpose of part 2 is to have students discuss examples of bullying. Through these discussions, they will define bullying, understand the Bullying Circle, and identify rules against bullying.

Journal Entries

1. Introduce the journal entries by telling the students that although these entries are about fictional students, bullying instances like these happen to students every day. Hand out a set of Session 1 Journal Entries to each student.

2. Explain to the students:

   We are going to start talking about cyber bullying by figuring out what bullying is and how students may be involved in it. We will read some journal entries from some students like you.

3. After the journal entries have been read, divide the class into small groups and assign one peer leader to each small group. Designate an area in the room where each small group will meet. They will meet in the same area for every session of the program.

4. Explain to the students:

   The small group you are now in will be the group you will stay with for this entire unit on cyber bullying prevention. You will meet in the same place every time. Each small group will be assigned one of the journal entries. The peer leader in your group will lead you in a discussion to talk about the questions about that entry, and then you will report back to the whole class.

TEACHER TIP
An alternative to paper and pencil journal entries would be to post these on a blog or message board accessible only to you and your students. This will help extend the learning. Suggestions for online homework using these online journal entries are included at the end of this session.

TEACHER TIP
You could also ask students to read the journal entries aloud. Be sure to choose students who can read expressively, or give the entries to them ahead of time so they are familiar with the material. You could also assign this reading to the peer leaders.

TEACHER TIP
Decide on the size and makeup of the small groups based on how your students work together and how many students you think will be manageable for the peer leaders to direct. The younger the students, (middle school, for example), the smaller the groups should be. If you are aware of students who have a history of bullying or being bullied, make sure they are not in the same group, so they feel comfortable talking about their experiences.

5. Assign each small group one of the student characters. If there are more than four small groups, two groups can work on the journal entry of the same character.

6. Allow 7 to 10 minutes for small groups to discuss the questions for the character they are assigned.

7. When the groups are ready, call on the peer leaders to read aloud to the class their groups' answers to the questions. Call on all the groups who discussed the same character together so you can summarize their answers and add comments according to the suggestions below.

Here are some suggested comments you can use to summarize each journal entry:

Character: Allie

Summarize by including these points:

Definition of *bullying*: Bullying occurs when someone repeatedly and on purpose says or does mean or hurtful things to another person who has a hard time defending himself or herself (Olweus et al. 2007).

Bullying is aggressive and unwanted behavior.

Bullying involves a pattern of behavior that is repeated over time.

Bullying involves an imbalance of power or strength. The power could be physical, emotional, social, or economic.

Teasing can be playful or friendly. But if it is degrading and offensive or if the teaser has been told to stop, it can become bullying if it continues.

TEACHER TIP
Throughout the curriculum as students report back about their discussions, you may need to guide or reframe their answers to correct misconceptions as as they arise.

Character: J.T.

Summarize by including these points:

There are many different kinds of bullying:

- **verbal bullying, such as name calling and making derogatory comments**
- **physical bullying, such as hitting, kicking, shoving, and spitting**
- **making threats or forcing someone to do something**
- **exclusion, which is leaving someone out or excluding them from a social group**
- **rumor spreading or lying**
- **theft and extortion of money or property, or damaging property**
- **racial bullying***
- **sexual harassment***
- **cyber bullying through the use of technology and Internet communication**

Bullying can be direct or indirect. It can be to someone's face or it can be behind the person's back, such as spreading rumors about someone or sending text messages about someone to others.

---

* These behaviors go beyond bullying and may be illegal.

Character: Serena

Summarize by including these points:

These are the four rules to prevent bullying that are used in the *Olweus Bullying Prevention Program (OBPP)* (Olweus et al. 2007):*

- **We will not bully others. (Bullying is not acceptable.)**

- **We will try to help students who are bullied. (We can do this by finding an adult to help, defending the student who is bullied, or befriending a student who is bullied.)**

- **We will try to include students who are left out. (Students who are bullied are often excluded.)**

- **If we know that somebody is being bullied, we will tell an adult at school and an adult at home. (Telling is not snitching** [*or use the term commonly used by your students*]; **it is following the rule that no bullying is allowed and may prevent someone from being hurt either physically or emotionally. Telling takes courage.)**

Display the Four Anti-Bullying Rules sheet.

Character: Aaron

Summarize by including these points:

Everyone who sees or is involved in a bullying situation plays a part in it and is affected by it.

The roles people play in bullying situations depend on their attitudes (positive, neutral, or negative) and their actions or behaviors (joining in, watching, helping).

---

*If you are already implementing *OBPP*, this discussion will be a review. If not, adopt these rules in your classroom, and encourage your administrators to consider adopting these rules schoolwide.

The different roles people play in bullying situations are called the Bullying Circle (Olweus et al. 2007). **The Bullying Circle includes these participants:**

- **person or persons who are bullying**
- **person who is bullied**
- **followers of the person doing the bullying who get involved but are not the ones who start it**
- **supporters who support the bullying but don't actually join in, who might laugh or encourage the person who is bullying**
- **passive supporters who like the bullying but don't show it**
- **onlookers who don't do anything positive or negative**
- **possible defenders who don't like the bullying and think they should do something to help but do nothing**
- **defenders who try to help the person who is being bullied**

Show the Bullying Circle diagram as you talk about each role.

8. Summarize the activity by saying:

You have probably all found yourselves playing some role in a bullying situation—even if it was as a bystander. From now on, our class (or *whole school*) **will start using these rules against bullying. This means that even if you just happen to be there, you should try to help. Don't be afraid to speak up if you see bullying behavior on school grounds. Telling an adult can prevent someone from getting into trouble or getting hurt. If you feel that you may be harmed by stepping in and helping, telling an adult can help stop the bullying too.**

Real-Life Story

1. When you introduce the real-life stories, let students know that each story is based on an actual event, but names and other facts have been changed and the points of view have been dramatized.

2. Hand out the Session 1 Real-Life Story to each small group.

3. Explain to the students:

We are going to start talking about cyber bullying by first figuring out what roles people play in bullying situations. Before we do that, let's refresh our memories on the definition of *bullying*:

Bullying occurs when someone repeatedly and on purpose says or does mean or hurtful things to another person who has a hard time defending himself or herself (Olweus et al. 2007).

There are several parts people play in a traditional bullying incident. These roles make up the Bullying Circle:

- **person or persons who are bullying**
- **person who is bullied**
- **followers of the person who is bullying who get involved but are not the ones who start it**
- **supporters who support the bullying but don't actually join in, who might laugh or encourage the person who is bullying**
- **passive supporters who like the bullying but don't show it**
- **onlookers who don't do anything positive or negative**

TEACHER TIP
An alternative to paper and pencil real-life stories would be to post these on a blog or message board accessible only to you and your students. This will help extend the learning. Suggestions for online homework using this real-life story are included at the end of this session.

- possible defenders who don't like the bullying and think they should do something to help but do nothing

- defenders who try to help the person who is being bullied

Show the Bullying Circle diagram as you talk about each role.

With the definition of *bullying* and the Bullying Circle in mind, let's read today's real-life story.

At the beginning of each story is a paragraph describing the incident. The teacher should read that aloud to students. Then each story includes at least two points of view. Ask for volunteers to each read one point of view aloud until all the views have been read.

TEACHER TIP
Decide on the size and makeup of the small groups based on how your students work together and how many students you think will be manageable for the peer leaders to direct. If you are aware of students who have a history of bullying or being bullied, make sure they are not in the same group, so they feel comfortable talking about their experiences.

4. After the real-life story has been read, divide the class into small groups and assign one peer leader to each small group. Designate an area in the room where each small group will meet. The groups will meet in the same areas for every session of the program.

5. Explain to the students:

   The small group you are now in will be the group you will stay with for this entire unit on cyber bullying prevention. You will meet in the same place every time. Each small group will receive a copy of the day's real-life story with some questions. The peer leader in your group will lead you in a discussion to talk about the questions and then you will report back to the whole class.

6. Allow 7 to 10 minutes for small groups to discuss the questions relating to the story.

7. After the allotted time, call the class back to order. Assign each group a question to answer first in front of the group to spark discussion. (If there are more groups than questions, double-up groups on a question and allow all of them to read

TEACHER TIP
Throughout the curriculum as students report back about their discussions, you may need to guide or reframe their answers to correct misconceptions as they arise.

TEACHER TIP
Olweus is pronounced Ol-vay-us.

their responses first.) After the designated group has given its answers, invite other groups to respond and give their answers. Some answers may be repeated, but this format will allow thoughtful discussion.

8. Explain to the students:

   Bullying is so prevalent that there are prevention programs out there for schools to implement. One such program is the *Olweus Bullying Prevention Program*. Within this program is the opportunity and suggestion to implement these Four Anti-Bullying Rules:*

   - **We will not bully others.**
   - **We will try to help students who are bullied.**
   - **We will try to include students who are left out.**
   - **If we know that somebody is being bullied, we will tell an adult at school and an adult at home.**

   Optional: Display the Four Anti-Bullying Rules sheet.

9. Summarize the activity by saying:

   You have probably all found yourselves playing some role in a bullying situation—even if it was as a bystander. From now on, keep these rules in mind. Don't be afraid to speak up if you see some bullying behavior on school grounds. Our next activity will help us internalize these rules and help out another school at the same time.

---

*Alternate language if your school is already implementing *OBPP*:
As you know, our school is implementing the *Olweus Bullying Prevention Program*. As part of this program, our school has adopted these Four Anti-Bullying Rules.

■ Cyber Bullying

PART 3
20 minutes

▶ **Creating Anti-Bullying Collages and Posters**

The purpose of part 3 is to help students remember and understand the rules to prevent bullying. Middle school students will create collages that will establish the classroom as a "no bullying allowed" environment. High school students will create posters of these rules to donate to an elementary school in the district.

Collages

TEACHER TIP
Students can work on their collages or posters in their peer-led small groups or in pairs.

1. Explain to the students:

   The four rules to prevent bullying will become part of our class rules. To remember them and think about what they mean, you will be creating word collages about each rule.

TEACHER TIP
You should have magazines, newspapers, or other print materials available for students to use in their collages and posters. They can also use other art materials that are available, such as markers, colored pencils or pens, crayons, scissors, glue sticks, and colored paper.

   Assign each group one of the Four Anti-Bullying Rules. Also give each group a piece of paper or poster board. Leave the Four Anti-Bullying Rules sheet displayed, so students can copy the rules onto their papers. Then have each group come up with words and phrases that apply to the rule or that are associated with the rule. The collages will be posted to remind students of these rules for the class.

2. Explain what other art materials could be used and that the materials should be shared among the groups or pairs.

3. Allow time for the groups or pairs to work on their collages. If time permits, have students show their collages to the rest of the class. When the collages are finished, post them in your classroom.

Posters

1. Explain to the students:

   As you know, the four rules to prevent bullying are a huge part of the *Olweus Bullying Prevention Program*. This program is usually done in elementary and middle schools. But that doesn't mean that we can't keep these rules in mind as we go about our lives here in our high school. To help us remember them and to help students at the elementary schools in our district, we are going to create posters of each rule to donate to one of the elementary schools.

   Split the class into four groups. Assign each group one of the Four Anti-Bullying Rules. Give each group a piece of poster board and art supplies.

2. Have each group look through newspapers and magazines, cutting out letters, words, and pictures to create posters that state the rules.

3. Allow time for the groups to work on their posters. If time permits, have students show their posters to the rest of the class. When the posters are finished, donate them to an elementary school in your district.

TEACHER TIP
Instead of creating posters with paper and glue, groups could create them on the computer and print them out.

■ Cyber Bullying

▶ **Conclusion and Homework Assignment**

1. Wrap up by inviting student volunteers to define *bullying* and the roles people play in the Bullying Circle.

   Today we learned what bullying is and how we can all be a part of it even if we're not the one who starts it. We're also trying to stop it by using rules to prevent bullying in our classroom.

   Call on students to repeat the rules against bullying:

   - We will not bully others.

   - We will try to help students who are bullied.

   - We will try to include students who are left out.

   - If we know that somebody is being bullied, we will tell an adult at school and an adult at home.

Wrap up by inviting student volunteers to define bullying and the roles people play in the Bullying Circle.

After today's activities, we all have a better understanding of what bullying is and how harmful it can be. Although we are donating the posters you created to an elementary school, the rules we worked with are something we should keep in mind for how we conduct ourselves here at *(insert name of your school)*.

2. Explain:

   Next time we will begin to talk about cyber bullying, what it is, and what we can do about it.

3. Hand out Homework Assignment 1. Explain to the students:

This homework assignment is for you to do with your parent or an adult you live with. If it is not possible for an adult you live with to do it with you, then another adult, like a relative or neighbor, could. If you have trouble finding an adult to work with, come and see me, and I will help you.

You will have five of these homework assignments during the program. Each one will have background information from the session for your parents or another adult to read through. It also has activities for you to do with that person, which will give you a chance to teach the adult what you learned and to hear what he or she thinks about it. These are the activities this week:

- **The adult shares a bullying experience from his or her youth with you.**

- **You both look at some bullying prevention Web sites or do an Internet search for bullying stories together.**

If you do not have access to the Internet, you can visit a library and do this assignment there. If this is not possible, look through newspapers and magazines for articles about bullying.

When you and the adult you are working with have finished the homework assignment, both of you need to sign the return slip on the last page and you will bring that part back. You will be graded on this assignment.

4. If you are posting the journal entries online, have students read through today's entries again and answer these questions online:

> What, if any, bullying situations have you seen or been a part of at school that are like the ones described in the journal entries?

Caution students not to use names or too many details.

 If you are posting the real-life stories online, have students read through today's story again and answer this question online:

> Why might popular students like Todd think that the bullying they are doing is not bullying but playing a joke or pulling a prank?

 5. Show the students where to put their homework slips.

6. Explain how students will be graded on this homework assignment.

7. Tell the students when the homework assignment will be due.

The definition of bullying, the Bullying Circle, and the Four Anti-Bullying Rules are used with permission from *Olweus Bullying Prevention Program: Teacher Guide,* by Dan Olweus, Susan P. Limber, et al., Hazelden Publishing, 2007.

SESSION 2

What Is Cyber Bullying?

Description

Through student journal entries or a real-life story, small- and large-group discussions, and a board game, students will understand what cyber bullying is and is not, and the technologies used to cyber bully.

Learner Outcomes

By the end of this session, students will be able to

- define *cyber bullying*.
- identify the technologies used in cyber bullying.
- identify cyber bullying situations.

Materials Needed

☐ CD-ROM materials:

Grade 6–8
- Session 2 Journal Entries S2-1

Grade 9–12
- Session 2 Real-Life Story S2-1

- Is It or Isn't It? game board, one per small group S2-4
- Is It or Isn't It? game cards, one set per small group S2-5
- Is It or Isn't It? Peer Leader Instructions S2-3

SESSION 2 AT A GLANCE

Total Time: 50 minutes

Part 1:
Journal Entries/ Real-Life Story and Discussion
(25 minutes)

Part 2:
Is It or Isn't It?
(20 minutes)

Part 3:
Conclusion and Homework Assignment
(5 minutes)

TEACHER TIP

Before teaching this session, be sure to read the Introduction to Cyber Bullying (pages 11–17) and go through the Teacher Training Presentation on the CD-ROM. I-14

- Homework Assignment 2 S2-6 (SP)

☐ Scissors

☐ Blank paper, or real game pawns, one per student

☐ Pens or pencils

☐ Dice, one die per small group

☐ *Optional:* Computers

Preparation Needed

1. Print out the Session 2 Journal Entries, one set per student.

   Students will be working on the journal entries in their small groups. Each small group will work on a different characters and all students in that small group will need a copy of that character's journal entry. However, you may wish to give all students a copy of all four journal entries to follow along as they are read aloud. You may also want to have extra copies so that members of a small group could discuss a second character if they finish their work early.

2. Print out the Session 2 Real-Life Story, one copy per student.

TEACHER TIP
This lesson includes a lot to cover. Be mindful of your time or divide this lesson into two class periods.

3. Print out the Is It or Isn't It? game board, one board per group.

4. Print and cut out the Is It or Isn't It? game cards, one set per group.

5. Cut the blank paper into small game pieces, or use real game pawns, one per student.

6. Print out the Is It or Isn't It? Peer Leader Instructions, one for each peer leader.

7. Gather dice.

8. Print out Homework Assignment 2, one copy per student.

SESSION 2 OUTLINE

PART 1
25 minutes

▶ **Journal Entries/Real-Life Story and Discussion**

The purpose of part 1 is to have students discuss examples of cyber bullying to understand what cyber bullying is and what technologies can be used to cyber bully.

  Journal Entries

TEACHER TIP

Extend the lesson by having students keep their own journals about cyber bullying. These journals should be graded based on completion of the assignment rather than content. It is important that students know the journals will be turned in and the teacher will read them. If students wish to write about specific incidents that they want to keep confidential, they should not use names of students involved.

1. Explain to the students:

   Last session we talked about bullying. What are some examples of bullying?

   Allow time for students to respond.

   Now that we know more about what bullying is, we're going to learn what cyber bullying is. So that we don't get confused, we're going to call it *traditional bullying* when we talk about the kind of bullying that does not involve computers or cell phones, which we call *technology*. We'll use the term *cyber bullying* when technology is involved.

   You might already know of examples of cyber bullying, but you just don't realize it. Sadly, there are many ways to use technology in a harmful way. As you read about Allie, J.T., Serena, and Aaron, think about anything that you have heard about or gone through that might be similar to what happened with them.

2. Hand out the Session 2 Journal Entries to the class. Read the journal entries aloud or have students read them aloud as the rest of the class follows along.

■ Cyber Bullying

TEACHER TIP
An alternative to paper and pencil journal entries would be to post these on a blog or message board accessible only to you and your students. This will help extend the learning. Suggestions for online homework for these journal entries are included at the end of this session.

TEACHER TIP
If one group finishes its discussion before the others, those students could work on the discussion questions of a second character.

TEACHER TIP
Throughout the curriculum as students report back about their discussions, you may need to guide or reframe their answers to correct misconceptions as they arise.

3. After the journal entries have been read, divide the class into the same peer-led small groups they were in last session and have them go to their designated areas in the classroom.

Assign one of the Session 2 Journal Entries to each group, making sure each group has a different character than the one it worked on last time. If there are more than four small groups, two groups can work on the journal entry of the same character.

4. Allow 7 to 10 minutes for small groups to discuss the questions for the characters they are assigned.

5. Before the groups are called on to report to the class, make a chart on the board with the following headings:

Traditional bullying is...   Cyber bullying is...

When the students report back to the class, fill in the chart with characteristics of traditional bullying under the heading "Traditional bullying is..." and examples of cyber bullying under the heading "Cyber bullying is...." Keep in mind that many of the characteristics under each heading will be the same.

6. When the groups are ready, call on the peer leaders to read aloud to the class their groups' answers to the questions. Call on all the groups who discussed the same character together. Fill in the chart as the students read their answers.

 S2-2   Grade 9–12   **Real-Life Story**

1. Explain to the students:

   Last session, we talked about bullying. What are some examples of bullying?

58   Duplicating this page is illegal. Do not copy this material without written permission from the publisher.

Allow time for students to respond.

TEACHER TIP
An alternative to paper and pencil real-life stories would be to post these on a blog or message board accessible only to you and your students. This will help extend the learning. Suggestions for online homework involving this real-life story are included at the end of this session.

Now that we have a clearer understanding of what bullying is, we can start talking about what cyber bullying is. So that we don't confuse the two, we're going to use the term *traditional bullying* when we refer to the kind of bullying that does not involve technology. We'll use the term *cyber bullying* when technology is involved.

You might already know of examples of cyber bullying, but you just don't realize it. Unfortunately there are many ways to use technology in a negative way. As you read today's real-life story, think of any similar examples that you know about or may have even experienced.

2. Hand out the Session 2 Real-Life Story to the class. Choose students or ask for volunteers to read the sections of the story aloud.

3. After the real-life story has been read, divide the class into the same peer-led small groups and have them go to their designated areas in the classroom.

4. Allow 7 to 10 minutes for small groups to discuss the questions related to the story.

5. Before the groups are called on to report to the class make a chart on the board with the following headings:

Traditional bullying is…   Cyber bullying is…

When the students report back to the class, fill in the chart with characteristics of traditional bullying under the heading "Traditional bullying is…" and examples of cyber bullying under the heading "Cyber bullying is…." Keep in

■ Cyber Bullying

mind that many of the characteristics under each heading will be the same.

TEACHER TIP
Throughout the curriculum as students report back about their discussions, you may need to guide or reframe their answers to correct misconceptions as they arise.

6. When the groups are ready, call the class back to order. Assign each group a question to answer first in front of the group to spark discussion. (If there are more groups than questions, double-up groups on a question and allow all of the groups to read their responses before discussion.) After the designated group has given its answers, invite other groups to respond and give their answers. Some answers may be repeated, but this format allows thoughtful discussion.

Chart Summary

1. After all of the groups have reported back, summarize the information on the left side of the chart by including these examples and talking points:

   Cyber bullying can involve the following (Kowalski, Limber, and Agatston 2008):

   - **sending mean or offensive messages repeatedly through emails, instant messaging (IMing), text messages, cell phone messages, chat room posts, or social-networking Web site postings**

   - **playing an online game and ruining the game for others on purpose**

   - **sending put-downs and insults through emails or text messages**

   - **humiliating people through technology, for example, posting information that is not true, altering photos in an offensive way, or making fun of someone through statements, photos, or songs**

- creating Web sites designed to humiliate or embarrass others, such as "slam books" (Web sites that list students' names for other students to make mean comments about)

- sending messages as though they are from someone else, which usually happens by using the targeted student's password and sending mean, offensive, or inappropriate messages or comments so that the receiver thinks the targeted student sent them

- sharing personal, often embarrassing, information about someone that they would not want shared by forwarding an email or a photo to others

- tricking someone into sharing personal information and then telling others about it through emails or text messaging

- leaving someone out of a group by taking the person off buddy lists or leaving the person out of password-protected sites

- hitting or hurting someone while photographing or video-taping the person, usually with a cell phone, and then sending the photos or videos to others for amusement

- sending threats intending to harm someone or encouraging the person to commit suicide—which should be reported to an adult immediately

2. Reread the definition of *bullying* below and ask the students to come up with their own definition of *cyber bullying*:

   Bullying occurs when someone repeatedly and on purpose says or does mean or hurtful things to another person who has a hard time defending himself or herself (Olweus et al. 2007).

3. On the far right side of the chart, summarize the information by including these points:

- Both traditional bullying and cyber bullying are very harmful.

- Cyber bullying can reach and involve many people very quickly.

- People who might not bully someone face to face might cyber bully someone because they can't be seen and think they are anonymous.

- Traditional bullying involves an imbalance of power. The student who bullies often targets someone he or she thinks won't fight back. Because those who cyber bully think they can be anonymous, they might not really be more physically or socially powerful, but they can feel powerful by using technology.

- Traditional forms of bullying can cause physical harm and psychological harm. In most cases, cyber bullying causes psychological harm.

- Traditional bullying is usually limited to the people in the immediate area where the bullying is taking place. Cyber bullying can reach many people immediately—and often the student who is targeted doesn't know who is doing it.

- Traditional bullying usually has a time and place, such as during lunch on school grounds. Cyber bullying can happen anytime and anyplace. The targeted student may even be unaware that it is happening for a while.

- It is usually apparent who is doing traditional bullying. It is often difficult to find out who is cyber bullying.

- Both traditional bullying and cyber bullying are not allowed at our school or in our classroom.

Ask students to describe examples of cyber bullying that they know about without using names or giving too many details.

PART 2
20 minutes

▶ **Is It or Isn't It?**

The purpose of part 2 is for students to identify cyber bullying situations and to understand why these situations are considered cyber bullying and not just an online exchange or joke.

📄 S2-3 through S2-5

Option 1: Play the paper version of the game.

1. Explain:

TEACHER TIP
It is recommended that you review the game cards before playing the game in class to make sure all the cards are appropriate for your students' age level.

We will now play a game in your small groups to help you identify what kinds of situations and online communications could be considered cyber bullying. Sometimes it's hard to tell. What you think is a joke might not be funny to someone else.

2. Explain the directions of the game:

I will give each small group a game board, game pawns, a die, and game cards. Each group's peer leader will have the game directions.

Each player will shake the die and move the number of spaces shown on the die. The player will then do whatever it says on the space where the pawn lands.

If the player lands on a space that reads "Is it or isn't it?" the peer leader will draw a card and read a situation to the player. The player will give two reasons they think that situation is or isn't cyber bullying.

The peer leader will then read the answer from the bottom of the card. If the player is correct, he or she will move ahead two spaces. If incorrect, the player will not move. If the player gives an answer that isn't included on the card, the group can vote on the appropriateness of the answer. When it is the peer leader's turn, the peer leader will ask another player to read the card and the answer.

■ Cyber Bullying

It's true that some situations might not be cyber bullying. But keep in mind that if someone sends you a message and you're not sure how to take it because you can't see the person's face, you need to clarify the message with that person to find out what was really meant.

The winner is the player who reaches the finish line first.

3. Give the small groups their game materials. Give a game pawn or piece to each student. If using paper, have each student write his or her name on the game piece.

4. Allow 10 to 15 minutes to play the game.

Remove and do not play the cards that are *not* examples of cyber bullying for this age level.

Option 2: If you have access to a computer, you might want to invite the students to create and play an online version of this game instead of using the paper game.

PART 3
5 minutes

▶ **Conclusion and Homework Assignment**

1. Explain:

   You now have a good idea of what cyber bullying is and how harmful it can be. What are some ways that people can be cyber bullied?

   Possible answers include repeatedly sending mean or offensive emails, IMs, and/or text messages; posting embarrassing information about someone else on a Web site; leaving someone out of a group or buddy/friends list; and sending messages as though they were from someone else.

   Cyber bullying is not a joke or just something that everybody does. It's something to take seriously.

   What is something you learned today about cyber bullying that you had not realized before?

   Allow several students to answer this question.

2. Summarize by saying:

   It's important that everyone understands what cyber bullying is and how harmful it can be. Share what you learned today with a friend.

(SP) S2-6

3. Hand out Homework Assignment 2. Explain to the students:

   This homework assignment is for you to do with your parent or an adult that you live with. If it is not possible for an adult you live with to do it with you, then another adult, such as a relative or neighbor, could. If you have trouble finding an adult to work with, come and see me, and I will help you. These are the activities for this week:

- There is some information for the adult to read.

- You both take a True/False Technology Quiz in an attempt to see who knows more and what you can learn from each other.

When you and the adult you are working with have completed the homework assignment, both of you need to sign the return slip at the bottom of the sheet and you will bring that part back to class. You will be graded on this assignment.

If you are posting the journal entries online, have students read through today's entries again and answer these questions online:

> Which do you think would be harder, being cyber bullied or being the friend who is unable to help the person being cyber bullied? Why?

If you are posting the real-life stories online, have students read through today's story again and answer these questions online:

> Have you ever been or known someone who has been excluded from your online community? What happened? How was the situation resolved?

4. Show the students where to put their homework slips.

5. Explain how students will be graded on this homework assignment.

6. Tell the students when the homework assignment will be due.

SESSION 3

How Does Cyber Bullying Affect People?

Description

Through student journal entries or a real-life story and group discussion, students will understand the serious effects of cyber bullying. Students will also develop a positive text-message language to explore how to use technology in a positive way.

Learner Outcomes

By the end of this session, students will be able to

- identify the effects of cyber bullying on the student who is bullied, on bystanders, and on the students who bully.
- identify how to use technology in a positive way.

Materials Needed

☐ CD-ROM materials:

- **Grade 6–8** Session 3 Journal Entries S3-1
- **Grade 9–12** Session 3 Real-Life Story S3-2
- Text Talk worksheet S3-3
- Homework Assignment 3 S3-4 (SP)

☐ Magazines or newspapers

☐ One sheet of poster board

SESSION 3 AT A GLANCE

Total Time: 50 minutes

Part 1:
Journal Entries/
Real-Life Story
and Discussion
(15 minutes)

Part 2:
Understanding
Empathy
(15 minutes)

Part 3:
Text-Messaging
Game
(15 minutes)

Part 4:
Conclusion
and Homework
Assignment
(5 minutes)

■ *Cyber Bullying*

☐ Scissors

☐ Glue

Preparation Needed

 1. Print out the Session 3 Journal Entries, one set per student.

   Students will be working on the journal entries in their small groups. Each small group will work on a different characters and all students in that small group will need a copy of that character's journal entry. However, you may wish to give all students a copy of all four journal entries to follow along as they are read aloud. You may also want to have extra copies so that members of a small group could discuss a second character if they finish their work early.

2. Print out the Session 3 Real-Life Story, one copy per student.

3. Print out the Text Talk worksheet, one copy per small group.

4. Print out Homework Assignment 3, one copy per student.

5. Look through the magazines or newspapers to find and cut out pictures of the following: a person (could be a celebrity), a group of friends, a school, someone laughing, a key, and a house. Lightly glue the picture of the person in the middle of the poster board and glue the rest of the pictures around the person. Label the pictures in this manner:

Image	Label
Person	Self-Esteem
Group of Friends	Friends
School	School/Learning
Laughing Person	Happiness
Key	Safety
House	Home/Family

How Does Cyber Bullying Affect People?

SESSION 3 OUTLINE

PART 1
15 minutes

▶ **Journal Entries/Real-Life Story and Discussion**

The purpose of part 1 is to have students understand how cyber bullying affects all the players in the Bullying Circle.

S3-1 Grade 6–8

Journal Entries

1. Explain to the students:

   During the last session, we learned what cyber bullying is. Who can refresh our memories as to what it is?

   Allow time for students to respond.

   We also started talking about how it can affect the person who is being cyber bullied. What do you think is happening to Allie from the Session 2 Journal Entries? Would this be cyber bullying?

TEACHER TIP
An alternative to paper and pencil journal entries would be to post these on a blog or message board accessible only to you and your students. This will help extend the learning. Suggestions for online homework related to these journal entries are included at the end of this session.

2. Hand out the Session 3 Journal Entries to the class. Read the journal entries or have students read them aloud as the rest of the class follows along.

3. After the journal entries have been read, divide the class into the peer-led small groups and have them go to their designated areas in the classroom.

   Assign journal entry characters to each small group, making sure each group has a different character than the one it worked on last time. If there are more than four small groups, two groups can work on the journal entry of the same character.

Duplicating this page is illegal. Do not copy this material without written permission from the publisher.

69

■ Cyber Bullying

TEACHER TIP
If one group finishes its discussion before the others, those students could work on the discussion questions of a second character.

4. Allow 7 to 10 minutes for small groups to discuss the questions for the characters they are assigned.

5. When the groups are ready, call on the peer leaders to read aloud to the class their groups' answers to the questions. Call on all of the groups who discussed the same character together. As students report back about their discussions, you may need to guide or reframe their answers to correct misconceptions as they arise.

  Real-Life Story

1. Explain to the students:

   During the last session, we learned what cyber bullying is. Who can refresh our memories as to what it is?

   Allow time for students to respond.

   We also started talking about how it can affect the person who is being cyber bullied. As we read today's real-life story, think of how all of the students involved might be affected.

TEACHER TIP
An alternative to paper and pencil real-life stories would be to post these on a blog or message board accessible only to you and your students. This will help extend the learning. Suggestions for online homework related to the real-life story are included at the end of this session.

2. Hand out the Session 3 Real-Life Story to the class. Choose students or ask for volunteers to read the sections of the story aloud.

3. After the real-life story has been read, divide the class into the same peer-led small groups and have them go to their designated areas in the classroom.

4. Allow 7 to 10 minutes for groups to discuss the questions related to the story.

5. When the groups are ready, call the class back to order. Assign each group a question to answer first in front of the entire group to spark discussion. (If there are more groups than questions, double-up groups on a question and allow all

of them to read their responses before discussing.) After the designated group has given its answers, invite other groups to respond and give their answers. Some answers may be repeated, but this format allows thoughtful discussion.

Grade 9–12

Discussion Summary

1. Summarize by saying:

    Everyone has the right to live his or her life without being bullied or harassed by someone else. It is important to understand that even if someone cyber bullies another person as a joke, it may not be a joke to the person who is being bullied.

    A common excuse is "I was only kidding." This excuse will not be accepted here, especially if the behavior harms the person it was meant for. The most important thing we should think about is how the bullied student is affected. This is where our concern should be.

    Cyber bullying can be so devastating that occasionally students have suffered from depression as a result, whether or not someone was "only kidding." Some students who have been cyber bullied have even died by suicide.

    Cyber bullying can also affect other people in the Bullying Circle. People who see it happening to others might be afraid it will happen to them. Some might feel pressured to join in when they don't want to. A school environment in which cyber bullying or any kind of bullying is taking place is not one that feels like a safe, friendly community.

    Those students who bully and are allowed to continue their behavior are also affected. As they get older, these students are more likely to get into other types of trouble and even commit crimes.

■ Cyber Bullying

PART 2
15 minutes

▶ **Understanding Empathy**

The purpose of this activity is to have students understand what empathy is and to think about what it would be like to be cyber bullied.

1. Explain:

   You have heard many examples of cyber bullying so far. Now we are going to look at some things that are important to people your age and see how these things might be affected if you were cyber bullied.

2. Display the prepared poster board.

TEACHER TIP
Some questions may not be appropriate for your class or grade level. Use your discretion about which questions to ask.

3. Ask the questions below to get students thinking about how all these things would be affected if they were cyber bullied. Ask at least three questions for each category. As the students talk about the negative effects, gradually tear that image off the poster. At the end of the discussion there should be nothing left of the pictures—only the labels should remain.

Self-Esteem

- How might being cyber bullied affect how you feel about yourself?

- How would you feel about yourself if someone you knew were sending you mean messages?

- How would you feel if you were getting hurtful emails or text messages and you didn't know who sent them?

Friends

- How would you feel about your friends if they were sending nasty emails about you?
- How would you feel about your friends if they were excluding you?
- How would you feel about your friends if they were sharing personal information about you?
- How would you feel about your friends if you didn't know who was bullying you?

School/Learning

- How would you feel if everyone at school saw a Web site that made fun of you?
- How would you feel if someone sent an embarrassing or insulting picture of you electronically to the whole school?
- How would you feel about going to school if your name were on a Web page where people made mean comments about you?
- Why could being cyber bullied affect someone's grades and how well the person does in school?

Happiness

- How might being cyber bullied affect how happy you are?
- Why might people who are cyber bullied feel depressed?
- Why might people who are cyber bullied feel anxious or nervous?

Cyber Bullying

Safety

- How would you feel if someone anonymous was sending you pornographic photos?

- How safe would you feel if you kept getting text messages making fun of your weight or height or some aspect of your appearance?

- How much could you trust people at school if you didn't know who was pretending to be you and making comments on other people's profiles?

- How would you feel if you got hate messages referring to your sexuality?

- How would you feel if you got hate messages referring to your race?

Home/Family

- How would your interaction with your family members be affected if you were being cyber bullied and were afraid to or didn't want to tell them?

- How would your family react if you were moody and depressed or sad?

- How would your family feel if they viewed a Web site with negative or nasty comments posted about you on the site?

4. After the pictures have been ripped off the poster board, explain:

Many teens who are cyber bullied would like to disappear, just like the pictures did. They feel so bad that they don't want to go to school or be with other teens because their reputations have been damaged.

5. Ask if anyone knows what the word *empathy* means. Allow several students to try to explain the definition.

6. Then summarize their suggestions and provide this definition:

   Empathy means understanding how someone else feels in a certain situation.

7. Explain:

   If you can empathize as you just did, then you can understand how harmful cyber bullying can be. Even if you think it's just a joke, think about how the other person will feel first.

■ Cyber Bullying

PART 3
15 minutes

▶ **Text-Messaging Game**

The purpose of part 3 is to help students build empathy and caring feelings toward others by using cyber technology in a positive way.

1. Explain:

   Now that we have talked about all the negative effects of cyber bullying, let's think about the ways we can have positive interactions using technology. For example, text messaging has its own language. There are abbreviations for everything!

   Invite students to share some of the abbreviations they use while text messaging, but ask them to keep it clean.

   There are even abbreviations for swear words, insults, and put-downs. You might even know more negative abbreviations than positive abbreviations!

   Today you will have a chance to come up with some new, more positive text abbreviations that I hope you can use in your own messages. Each small group will be challenged to come up with at least five new positive text abbreviations. I will collect all your ideas at the end of class and make a list to hand out to everyone, so you can use these positive messages when you are texting each other.

   S3-3

2. Have students rejoin their peer-led groups. Give each peer leader a Text Talk worksheet to fill out with his or her group.

3. Explain:

   Each peer leader should write the new abbreviations in the left-hand column on the sheet and their meanings in the

How Does Cyber Bullying Affect People?

right-hand column. Remember, these messages can only be positive. Here's an example:

ULG2D means "You look great today!"

TEACHER TIP

For a quick game, have the groups exchange lists, or give out the whole list generated by all the groups without including the meanings and invite students to try to figure out what the new abbreviations mean. Follow up this guessing game by giving the students a complete list with all the meanings.

4. Allow approximately 10 minutes for the groups to work.

5. When the groups have finished, ask the peer leaders to share some of their groups' new abbreviations, as time permits.

6. Collect the sheets and combine the new words into one list to give students during your next session. Encourage students to use these new positive abbreviations when text messaging each other.

■ Cyber Bullying

▶ **Conclusion and Homework Assignment**

1. Explain:

    Invite student volunteers to explain the definition of *empathy* and some of the effects that cyber bullying has on those involved.

    Technology can help us do things faster, easier, and sometimes better. But if it's abused, it can have serious consequences. Remember the new positive text-message abbreviations you made today and use them with your friends.

2. Hand out Homework Assignment 3. Explain to the students:

    This homework assignment is for you to do with your parent or an adult that you live with. If it is not possible for an adult you live with to do it with you, then another adult, such as a relative or neighbor, could. If you have trouble finding an adult to work with, come and see me, and I will help you. These are the activities this week:

    • **The adult has some information to read.**

    • **You both will go through the ABC's of Cyber Bullying Prevention, which will give you ideas about ways to prevent or stop cyber bullying.**

    When you and the adult you are working with have completed the homework assignment, both of you need to sign the return slip at the bottom of the sheet and you need to bring that part back.

If you are posting the journal entries online, have students read through today's entries again and answer this question online:

> How is what is happening to Allie like what is happening to Mrs. Vargo?

If you are posting the real-life stories online, have students read through today's story again and answer this question online:

Why might some people think that watching and forwarding links to this video is *not* cyber bullying?

  3. Show the students where to put their homework slips.

4. Explain how students will be graded on this homework assignment.

5. Tell the students when the homework assignment will be due.

SESSION 4

Why Do People Cyber Bully Others?

Description

Through journal entries or a real-life story and small- and large-group discussions, students will understand why teens cyber bully others. Then through the creation of public service announcements (PSAs), students will take steps to prevent cyber bullying and take a stand against it.

Learner Outcomes

By the end of this session, students will be able to

- identify reasons people think they can cyber bully others.
- state why they think cyber bullying is unacceptable.

Materials Needed

☐ CD-ROM materials:

- Session 4 Journal Entries S4-1

- Session 4 Real-Life Story S4-2

- PSA Planning Sheet S4-3

- Homework Assignment 4 S4-4 (SP)

SESSION 4 AT A GLANCE

Total Time: 50 minutes

Part 1:
Journal Entries/
Real-Life Story
and Discussion
(25 minutes)

Part 2:
Stop Cyber Bullying
(20 minutes)

Part 3:
Conclusion
and Homework
Assignment
(5 minutes)

■ Cyber Bullying

☐ Your school's policy(ies) on bullying or cyber bullying, if available

☐ Transparency and overhead projector, or a chalkboard and chalk

☐ Materials for PSAs, such as poster board, video cameras, CD recorders, depending on the type of PSAs students will be doing

Preparation Needed

1. Print out the Session 4 Journal Entries, one set per student.

TEACHER TIP
This lesson includes a lot of content to cover. Be mindful of your time or divide the session into two class periods.

Students will be working on the journal entries in their small groups. Each small group will work on a different characters and all students in that small group will need a copy of that character's journal entry. However, you may wish to give all students a copy of all four journal entries to follow along as they are read aloud. You may also want to have extra copies so that members of a small group could discuss a second character if they finish their work early.

2. Print out the Session 4 Real-Life Story, one copy per student.

3. Print out the PSA Planning Sheet, one copy per small group.

4. Print out the Homework Assignment 4, one copy per student.

5. Before class, check with your school administrator about what policy or policies are in place regarding cyber bullying and review the policies. If none are in place, maybe your class can lobby for some.

Why Do People Cyber Bully Others?

SESSION 4 OUTLINE

PART 1
25 minutes

▶ **Journal Entries/Real-Life Story and Discussion**

The purpose of part 1 is to give students an understanding of why people cyber bully others and why they think they can get away with it.

S4-1 Grade 6–8 **Journal Entries**

1. Explain to the students:

   During the last session, we talked about the effects of cyber bullying, especially on the person who is being cyber bullied. What are some of these possible effects?

   Allow several students to respond.

   Why do you think anybody would do something so mean that could cause so much pain to someone else? That's what Allie, J.T., Serena, and Aaron talk about in their journal entries today.

2. Hand out the Session 4 Journal Entries to the class. Read the journal entries or have students read them aloud as the rest of the class follows along.

3. After the journal entries have been read, divide the class into the same peer-led small groups and have them go to their designated areas in the classroom.

4. Assign one character in the journal entries to each small group, making sure each group has a different character than the one it worked on last time. If there are more than four small groups, two groups can work on the journal entry of the same character.

TEACHER TIP
An alternative to paper and pencil journal entries would be to post these on a blog or message board accessible only to you and your students. This will help extend the learning. Suggestions for online homework related to these journal entries are included at the end of this session.

■ Cyber Bullying

TEACHER TIP
If one group finishes its discussion before the others, those students could work on the discussion questions of a second character.

5. Allow 7 to 10 minutes for small groups to discuss the questions related to the characters they are assigned.

6. When the groups are ready, call on the peer leaders to read aloud to the class their groups' answers to the questions. Call on all of the groups who discussed the same character together. As the students report back, make a list on a chalkboard or overhead of the reasons people cyber bully when it is such a mean thing to do.

Real-Life Story

1. Explain to the students:

   During the last session, we talked about the effects of cyber bullying, especially on the person who is being cyber bullied. What are some of these possible effects?

   Allow several students to respond.

   Why do you think anybody would do something so mean that could cause so much pain to someone else? We will explore that question in our real-life story today.

TEACHER TIP
An alternative to paper and pencil real-life stories would be to post these on a blog or message board accessible only to you and your students. This will help extend the learning. Suggestions for online homework related to the real-life story are included at the end of this session.

2. Hand out the Session 4 Real-Life Story to the class. Choose students or ask for volunteers to read the sections of the story aloud.

3. After the real-life story has been read, divide the class into the same peer-led small groups and have them go to their designated areas in the classroom.

4. Allow 7 to 10 minutes for small groups to discuss the questions related to this story.

5. When the groups are ready, call the class back to order. Assign each group a question to answer first in front of the

group to spark discussion. (If there are more groups than questions, double-up groups on a question and allow all of them to read their responses before discussion.) After the designated group has given its answers, invite other groups to respond and give their answers. Some answers may be repeated, but this format allows thoughtful discussion.

As the students report back, make a list on a chalkboard or overhead transparency of the reasons people cyber bully when it is such a mean thing to do.

Discussion Summary

1. Summarize students' answers by including these points:

   People may cyber bully because

   - **they think people won't know who they are; they can be anonymous.**
   - **they can't be seen.**
   - **they don't have to see the other person's reactions.**
   - **they think everybody does it, so it's no big deal.**
   - **they like making someone else feel bad.**

   Even though many people who cyber bully think no one will know they did it, everything we ever do on a computer is recorded somewhere in the computer's hard drive. People call this *cyber footprints*. **These cyber footprints can be traced. People who cyber bully through text messaging can also be traced by their phone numbers.**

   Internet service providers (such as AOL or Comcast) and social-networking Web sites (like MySpace.com) can also trace messages. If a person sends an email message or posts a message on a social-networking Web site, the message can be

■ Cyber Bullying

traced to the person—even if he or she used a different screen name or sent something anonymously.

If people keep copies of the bullying messages they've received and are able to trace who sent them, the sender may end up in trouble with the law.

This happened to a sixteen-year-old boy in Georgia who used a screen name to send threatening messages and write threats on his MySpace account. Some students contacted the school and the police were called in. The student was identified and arrested after an investigation showed who he was.

2. Read and discuss your school's policy regarding cyber bullying, if available.

3. Project a blank transparency on an overhead projector or use a dry-erase board or chalkboard and write the following headings:

   A person who cyber bullies…   A person who doesn't
                                         cyber bully…

4. Ask:

   How do you think a person might feel about himself or herself and others if he or she chooses to cyber bully or join in cyber bullying others?

   Allow several students to answer this question. Write their answers in the left-hand column.

   Possible answers include that the person doesn't care about others, is jealous of others, always wants to get even, likes to tease people in mean ways, likes to hurt people's feelings, and likes to feel powerful.

5. Then in the right-hand column, generate a list of how a person who chooses not to cyber bully might feel about himself or herself and others.

   Possible answers include that the person knows how to empathize with others, is considerate of others, knows how to make friends, knows how to keep friends, knows how to interact well with others, knows how to deal with feelings, knows how to have fun, takes responsibility for his or her actions, knows how to make good decisions, and is someone people can trust.

6. Summarize by saying:

   If you are involved in cyber bullying or see it when you are online, think about the choices you want to make and how you want to treat others before you decide to join in. When you decide not to join in, think about whether there's anything you could do to stop it.

■ Cyber Bullying

PART 2
20 minutes

▶ **Stop Cyber Bullying**

The purpose of part 2 is for students to take a stand against cyber bullying in their school. The peer-led groups will be creating a public service announcement, or PSA. A PSA is a noncommercial advertisement usually made to raise awareness about an issue or cause.

The PSAs that students will create can take the form of a poster, an announcement over your school's public-address system, or a video shown on your school's closed-circuit TV system. If you are limited on time, having all students work on creating posters would be best.

Whatever format students decide to use, it is important that their PSAs be heard or seen, so students realize they are taking actual steps to stop or prevent cyber bullying. Depending on what medium your students use, you may need to include extra class time or have students continue their work in another class, such as an art or media class.

You might also assign portions of this project as a homework assignment. Another option would be to have students present their PSAs to each other when they present their final project to the whole class in session 8. You could also encourage students to hang their posters around the school, show their video PSAs over your closed-circuit TV system (if available), and read them over the PA system during morning or afternoon announcements.

1. Explain to the students:

    Now that you know a lot about what cyber bullying is, how it affects people, and why people might think they can get away with it, it's time to start doing something about it. How many of you know what a public service announcement is?

    A public service announcement, also called a PSA, is an advertisement that's not selling something. It's usually designed to get people thinking about an issue or cause.

TEACHER TIP
Prior to class, do an Internet search for PSAs about cyber bullying to see some examples.

In your small groups, you will create public service announcements about preventing or stopping cyber bullying.

You may have seen or heard similar announcements about smoking or drug prevention. They usually have a message and a clever or eye-catching way of getting that message across. Can you think of some PSAs that you have seen or heard recently on the television or on the radio? Have you seen any in newspapers and magazines?

2. Explain:

Each small group will use a planning sheet to plan your PSA. Then you will have an opportunity to create a PSA that you will present to other students at our school.

 S4-3

3. Give each peer leader a PSA Planning Sheet. Briefly go through the sheet by explaining:

The target audience is the group of people your PSA is intended to reach. Maybe you will want to make one that is aimed at girls your age or maybe you want to target boys and girls younger than you. It's up to your group to decide.

Decide what your message will be. You should be able to state this in one sentence, for example, "If you think no one knows you're cyber bullying, it's not true, because your computer keeps a record of everything you do."

TEACHER TIP
If students do not have a choice of the medium they can use, simply tell them what kind of PSA they will be creating.

Decide what medium you will use. Your choices are posters, videos, or audio, such as a PSA that could be heard on the radio or on our school's PA system.

Explain equipment use or availability if they are doing audio or video projects.

Describing the PSA means that you will outline or plan it. You should write a detailed description so it will be easy to create it from that description. For example, if you are making a poster, your description will explain what it looks like and what words will be on it. If you are creating a PSA for the radio, you will write the dialogue and who is speaking, just like a play script. If you are making a video, you will write what is happening in the scene, where it is taking place, what is being said, and who is saying it.

Decide who will do each part of the PSA. For example, who will be the printer, artist, actor, speaker, or cameraperson.

4. Tell each group that they will need to fill out the planning sheet and show it to you before they move to the next step of making the PSA.

5. Allow time for students to work on their PSAs, or assign portions of this work as a homework assignment.

6. If possible, have students show or present their PSAs to the rest of the class or to the school when they are finished, or during session 8.

PART 3
5 minutes

▶ **Conclusion and Homework Assignment**

1. Explain:

   Congratulations on taking steps to prevent cyber bullying in our school! You can also prevent cyber bullying by what you do (or don't do) when you see cyber bullying happening. For example, the next time you see a text message that you know is cyber bullying, take a stand.

   You can take a stand by not responding to the message or by not forwarding it to others. You can also take a stand by sending a message back telling the sender that cyber bullying is not okay or by reporting it to an adult. We will learn more about taking a stand during our next session.

2. Tell the students where their posters will be posted or when their PSAs will be heard or shown to the rest of the school or at least another class. Explore posting some at another school, a local library, mall, or other community setting to help raise awareness about cyber bullying.

3. Hand out Homework Assignment 4 to each student. Explain to the students:

   This is a homework assignment for you to do with a parent or another adult that you live with. If it is not possible for an adult you live with to do it with you, then another adult, such as a relative or neighbor, could do it with you. If you have trouble finding an adult to do it with you, come and see me, and I will help you. These are the activities this week:

   • The adult has some information to read.

   • You both make family rules about Internet use.

■ Cyber Bullying

When you and the adult you are working with have completed the homework assignment, both of you need to sign the return slip at the bottom of the sheet and you need to bring that part back to class.

 If you are posting the journal entries online, have students read through today's entries again and answer this question online:

> What is the difference between saying something mean to someone's face and using technology to send something mean to someone?

 If you are posting the real-life stories online, have students read through today's story again and answer these questions online:

> If you were to come across a Web site like the one Yvette created about Lucy, what would your reaction be? What could you do about it?

  4. Show the students where to put their homework slips.

5. Explain how students will be graded on this homework assignment.

6. Tell the students when the homework assignment will be due.

SESSION 5

How Should You React to Cyber Bullying?

Description

Through journal entries or a real-life story, small- and large-group discussions, and sample situations, students will learn what to do if someone cyber bullies them or someone else.

Learner Outcomes

By the end of this session, students will be able to

- identify what steps to take if they are cyber bullied.
- identify what steps to take if they know someone else is being cyber bullied.

Materials Needed

☐ CD-ROM materials:

- Session 5 Journal Entries S5-1

- Session 5 Real-Life Story S5-2

- Do First poster and handout I-15, S5-3

- Question Cube S5-4

- What Would You Do If…? situation sheet S5-5

- Homework Assignment 5 S5-6 (SP)

SESSION 5 AT A GLANCE

Total Time: 50 minutes

Part 1:
Journal Entries/
Real-Life Story
and Discussion
(25 minutes)

Part 2:
Practice Saying "No"
to Cyber Bullying
(20 minutes)

Part 3:
Conclusion
and Homework
Assignment
(5 minutes)

■ Cyber Bullying

☐ Chalkboard and chalk, or flipchart or poster board and markers

☐ Your school's bullying/cyber bullying policy, if available

☐ Scissors

☐ Clear tape

Preparation Needed

1. Print out the Session 5 Journal Entries, one set per student.

   Students will be working on the journal entries in their small groups. Each small group will work on a different characters and all students in that small group will need a copy of that character's journal entry. However, you may wish to give all students a copy of all four journal entries to follow along as they are read aloud. You may also want to have extra copies so that members of a small group could discuss a second character if they finish their work early.

2. Print out the Session 5 Real-Life Story, one copy per student.

3. Print out the Do First poster, enlarge and display it in your space

4. Print out the Do First handout, one copy per student.

5. Print out the Question Cubes, one per small group. Cut and assemble them. (This could also be done by the peer leaders.)

6. Select the situations for your classroom and print the What Would You Do If...? situation sheets, one set per small group.

7. Print out Homework Assignment 5, one copy per student.

How Should You React to Cyber Bullying?

SESSION 5 OUTLINE

PART 1
25 minutes

▶ **Journal Entries/Real-Life Story and Discussion**

The purpose of part 1 is to identify the steps to take if you or someone you know is being cyber bullied.

  Journal Entries

1. Explain to the students:

   During the last session, we talked about why people think they can get away with cyber bullying. What are some of the reasons?

   Allow time for students to respond.

   TEACHER TIP
   An alternative to paper and pencil journal entries would be to post the journal entries on a blog or message board accessible only to you and your students. This will help extend the learning. Suggestions for online homework related to the journal entries are included at the end of this session.

   You also did a good job of making PSAs so students in our school and people in our community are more aware of cyber bullying. Since we know that it does happen, today we will talk about what to do if cyber bullying happens to you, someone you know, or even someone you don't know. And we'll read more about Allie, J.T., Serena, and Aaron to see what happens.

2. Hand out the Session 5 Journal Entries to the class. Read the journal entries or have students read them aloud as the rest of the class follows along.

3. After the journal entries have been read, divide the class into the same peer-led small groups and have them go to their designated areas in the classroom.

4. Assign one character in the journal entries to each small group, making sure each group has a different character than

Duplicating this page is illegal. Do not copy this material without written permission from the publisher.

■ Cyber Bullying

TEACHER TIP
If one group finishes its discussion before the others, those students could work on the discussion questions of a second character.

TEACHER TIP
As students report back about their discussions, you may need to guide or reframe their answers to correct misconceptions as they arise.

the one it worked on last time. If there are more than four small groups, two groups can work on the journal entry of the same character. Have each small group discuss the questions related to its assigned character.

5. Allow 7 to 10 minutes for small groups to discuss the questions for the characters they are assigned.

6. When the groups are ready, call on the peer leaders to read aloud to the class their groups' answers to the questions. Call on all of the groups with the same character together.

  Real-Life Story

1. Explain to the students:

   During the last session, we talked about why people think they can get away with cyber bullying. What are some of the reasons?

   Allow time for students to respond.

   You also did a good job of making PSAs so students in our school and people in our community are more aware of cyber bullying. Since we know that cyber bullying does happen, today we will talk about what to do if cyber bullying happens to you, someone you know, or even someone you don't know. And we'll be reading another real-life story that will help us learn more.

TEACHER TIP
An alternative to paper and pencil real-life stories would be to post these on a blog or message board accessible only to you and your students. This will help extend the learning. Suggestions for online homework related to the story are included at the end of this session.

2. Hand out the Session 5 Real-Life Story to the class. Choose students or ask for volunteers to read the sections of the story aloud.

3. After the real-life story has been read, divide the class into the same peer-led small groups and have them go to their designated areas in the classroom.

4. Allow 7 to 10 minutes for the small groups to discuss the questions related to the story.

5. When the groups are ready, call the class back to order. Assign each group a question to answer first in front of the group to spark discussion. (If there are more groups than questions, double-up groups on a question and allow all of them to read their responses before discussion.) After the designated group has given its answers, invite other groups to respond and give their answers. Some answers may be repeated, but this format allows thoughtful discussion.

Discussion Summary: Do First

1. Write these two headings on a chalkboard, flipchart, or poster board:

   If you were cyberbullied...   If someone else were cyberbullied...

TEACHER TIP
Depending on students' answers, you may need to comment or gently guide students to more appropriate and safer solutions.

2. After students report back on their small-group discussions, ask them about what they could do if they or someone else they know were cyber bullied. List their ideas of what to do under each heading.

3. Summarize their answers by saying:

   You've already come up with some good ideas about what to do if you or someone you know is being cyber bullied. If it happens to you or a friend, or someone you know even if they're not your good friend, you will probably find it upsetting and wonder what you should do first. Here is a list to help you remember what to do or how to help someone else.

   You can remember this list using the acronym Do First. Each letter in these two words represents a step you can take to

address cyber bullying. As a friend of someone who is being cyber bullied, you could help that person remember these steps as well.

I-15
S5-3

4. Display the Do First poster. Distribute a copy of the Do First poster and handout to each student. Discuss the points on the poster using the language provided:

Do not retaliate. When people find out that something mean or nasty or untrue is being said about them, they often want to get back at whoever did it. Not only will that make things worse, but you will be giving the person who is cyber bullying what he or she wants—a reaction from you.

The people who are cyber bullying may think they have power over you because you can't see them, but they also can't see your reaction. Sometimes people bully others to make them mad and upset, so don't let them have their way. If you don't try to get back at them, they might think it didn't matter to you and may leave you alone. Also, if you do try to get back at them, the students who are cyber bullying could use what you did as evidence against you instead.

Off your buddy list! If you've been bullied through IMing or a social-networking Web site, such as MySpace.com or Xanga.com, take that screen name off your list so the person won't bother you any more. It's possible that the person may start to bully you with another user name or in another way, however, so be on the lookout.

Figure out who it is. If you've been bullied through text messages on your cell phone, you can trace the number through your phone. If you know who it is, you might decide to avoid that person if it's someone at school. Or you might think of a possible response—and this is different from retaliation. We'll talk more about this in a few minutes.

If you are receiving threatening email messages, these can be traced through your Internet service provider. You can get an adult to help you with this. Social-networking Web sites also have ways to trace these kinds of messages. If you are receiving messages or postings that threaten your safety or someone else's safety, you need to talk to an adult right away.

Ignore it. Sometimes just ignoring it makes the people who are cyber bullying stop, because their actions are not having the effect they're hoping for. If someone sends only one mean email, you can probably ignore it.

Respond after you think about it carefully. A response is different than retaliation. You might be hurt or angry or upset, but you don't want to give the people who are cyber bullying the satisfaction of knowing it. So if you choose to respond, make it clear and cool. Don't give the people who are bullying anything that could be used as bullying evidence against you.

Save the evidence! This is very important! Save anything that is harmful—even the messages you decided to ignore—in case you receive more of them later. If the bullying continues, you will need to have evidence before steps can be taken to make it stop. You can save evidence by printing it, copying and saving it, or just not erasing it.

Tell an adult! If you receive or are aware of threatening or disturbing messages, it is important that you tell an adult immediately. This could be an adult at school or an adult at home. Here at our school, we will take all reports of cyber bullying very seriously. Let's talk about who you might tell at our school.

Have a brief discussion that makes clear that students can tell you or any adult at school, but highlight any specific procedures your school has in place to report cyber bullying or bullying of any kind. You may also want to revisit your school's policy, if available.

There have been serious situations at some schools that might have been prevented if students had told someone about disturbing and threatening messages that they were aware of.

5. Remind students:

If you have a friend who is being cyber bullied, he or she will need your support. The person might also need your help deciding what to do. If you are encouraged to join in cyber bullying, or if someone sends you emails or messages about someone else, respond by saying that you think it's mean and you won't send it to anyone else. Because adults don't always know when cyber bullying is going on, you may need to tell them and ask them to help stop it.

How Should You React to Cyber Bullying?

PART 2
20 minutes

▶ **Practice Saying "No" to Cyber Bullying**

The purpose of part 2 is to give students the opportunity to practice how they would react to cyber bullying situations if they were cyber bullied, the friend of someone who was cyber bullied, or a bystander aware of a cyber bullying situation.

1. Explain to the students:

   You will now have a chance to practice using the Do First steps to figure out how to help someone who is being cyber bullied.

S5-4

TEACHER TIP
You may want to choose which situations you would like your class to discuss, depending on the age of your students and their experiences with cyber bullying in your community. To do this, copy only the situations you want to use and make your own What Would You Do If...? situation sheet.

- **Each small group will receive a Question Cube with questions on it.**

- **Each group's peer leader will read a situation, and you will take turns rolling the cube gently and answering the question that is on top.**

- **These questions are on the cube:**

  - **What would you do if this happened to you?**

  - **What would you do if this happened to a friend?**

  - **What would you do if you heard about it or saw it?**

  - **What would you do if you knew who did the bullying?**

  - **What would you do if this happened to someone you didn't like?** (This should not change how someone would act.)

- **And the cube includes a special situation question. This question at the end of the situation on the sheet is only about that particular situation.**

- **Two people might get the same question. Since they might do something different, they could answer the same question. If a question has been answered twice, the next**

student to get that question should roll the cube again for a new question.

- **After everyone in the group has had a turn, the peer leader will read the next situation.**

 S5-5

2. Hand out a What Would You Do If...? situation sheet to each peer leader.

3. Allow students 10 to 15 minutes for small groups to use the Question Cube to discuss their situations.

4. Circulate among the groups to monitor their discussions.

PART 3
5 minutes

▶ **Conclusion and Homework Assignment**

1. Ask:

   Which situations do you think might happen in this school? Were any of these situations similar to ones that you already know about?

   Allow time for discussion between questions.

2. Remind students about the Do First handout and tell them to keep this in a special place so they can refer to it as needed.

3. Hand out Homework Assignment 5. Explain to the students:

   This is a homework assignment for you to do with a parent or an adult you live with. If it is not possible for an adult you live with to do the assignment with you, then another adult, such as a relative or neighbor, could do it with you. If you have trouble finding an adult to do it with you, come and see me, and I will help you. These are the activities this week:

   • **The adult has some information to read.**

   • **You both make commitments to stop or prevent cyber bullying.**

   When you and the adult you are working with have completed the homework assignment, both of you need to sign the return slip at the bottom of the last page and you need to bring that part back to class.

If you are posting the journal entries online, have students read through today's entries again and tell them to do the following assignment online. If you are not posting the journal entries online, students will need to complete this assignment on paper and turn it in.

■ Cyber Bullying

TEACHER TIP
If time permits, you can briefly discuss these homework assignment paragraphs at the beginning of session 6. However, they should also be handed in for grading and feedback from you.

One of your homework assignments for this session will be to choose one of the two situations talked about in the journal entries—Aaron and the cyber bullying of his teacher or the situation with Allie, J.T., and Serena. Using what you've learned, especially the Do First steps, write a paragraph that explains how you would work out the situation in a positive and respectful way. This paragraph will be due at the next session on _____ *(insert date).*

If you are posting the real-life stories online, have students do the following assignment online. If you are not posting the real-life stories online, students will need to complete this assignment on paper and turn it in.

One of your homework assignments for this session will be to search online or in the newspaper for a story about cyber bullying. Using what you've learned, especially the Do First steps, write a paragraph that explains how you would resolve the situation in a positive and respectful way. This paragraph will be due at the next session on *(insert date).*

4. Show the students where to put their homework slips.

5. Explain how students will be graded on this homework assignment.

6. Tell the students when the homework will be due.

SESSION 6

Creating a Positive Cyber Site, Part I

Description

Through a small-group project, students will create plans for their own social-networking Web sites that will promote safe and positive Internet use.

Learner Outcomes

By the end of this session, students will be able to

- describe how some social-networking Web sites began.
- explain what social-networking Web sites do to curb abuse.
- describe the steps in planning a social-networking Web site.
- describe rules for belonging to some social-networking Web sites.

The small-group project of creating a plan for a social-networking Web site will be introduced in this session. Students will work in their peer-led small groups. The students will continue to work on this project during session 7. Each small group will give a 5-minute class presentation about its Web site during session 8. You may wish to give more class time to this project or assign some of the project work as homework.

SESSION 6 AT A GLANCE

Total Time: 50 minutes

Part 1:
Introduction
(15 minutes)

Part 2:
Getting Started
(30 minutes)

Part 3:
Conclusion
(5 minutes)

■ Cyber Bullying

Materials Needed

☐ CD-ROM materials:

- Xanga Terms of Use, Member Conduct S6-2
- Web Site Planning Packet S6-3
- Facts of the Feature sheet S6-4
- Session 6 Journal Entries S6-1

☐ Overhead projector and transparency paper, or computer and LCD projector

Preparation Needed

1. Print the Xanga information and make the transparencies. Or prepare it on PowerPoint slides.

2. Print out the Web Site Planning Packet, one copy per small group.

3. Print out the Facts of the Feature sheet, one or two copies per student.

4. Make copies the Session 6 Journal Entries, one set per student.

5. Visit some social-networking Web sites so you are familiar with their format and content.

SESSION 6 OUTLINE

PART 1
15 minutes

▶ **Introduction**

The purpose of part 1 is to introduce the small-group project in which students will create a plan for a social-networking Web site that promotes positive and safe Internet use.

TEACHER TIP
The written paragraphs from session 5 are due at this time. Collect or print them to read and comment on and/or have students read their paragraphs aloud, if time permits.

1. Explain to the students:

   Today we will talk about social-networking Web sites. What are some examples of social-networking Web sites you know of?

   Possible answers include MySpace, Facebook, Xanga, Friendster, Bebo, Vox, and Club Penguin.

2. Ask:

   Why do you think we should talk about these Web sites in a program about cyber bullying?

   One possible answer is because a lot of cyber bullying goes on through these sites.

   What are some examples of cyber bullying or inappropriate use of social-networking Web sites that you have seen or heard about?

   Caution students to not use names or too many details.

   What are some examples of positive ways to use these sites? What do you like about them?

   Allow time between questions for students to answer.

   What if you could create your own positive social-networking Web site? What kinds of features would you like to have on it? What would it look like?

■ Cyber Bullying

Allow time between questions for students to answer.

3. Summarize by saying:

You have a lot of good ideas. And actually that's how these sites started—a few people who knew computers had a lot of good ideas.

The following are examples of how certain sites began. Guess which sites they are.

Example 1:

Three guys who took digital photos and videos at a party wanted to figure out how they could download them and send them to their friends so they could see them without having a special software program. When they figured it out, what site did they create?

The answer is YouTube.

Example 2:

A man named Tom Anderson and some computer programmers set up this site in 2003. It allows people to share information about themselves. The Web site and the company that owned it were bought for $580 million dollars in 2005.

The answer is MySpace.

Example 3:

A college student started this site as a hobby and as a way for college students to share information about themselves. It spread to other colleges and eventually became what site?

The answer is Facebook.

Example 4:

What site began as a site for sharing book and music reviews?

The answer is Xanga.

Example 5:

What Web site was started by a company that makes stuffed animals?

The answer is Webkinz.

4. Ask:

   How do these sites make money if you don't pay for them?

   A possible answer is advertising. Also, companies want as many people as possible to see their advertisements, and they pay a lot of money to have them on sites that are very popular with an age group that has a lot of money—for example, tweens and teens!

5. Ask:

   Are there age limits for these sites?

   The answer is yes, most have age limits, but these can be difficult to enforce.

6. Ask:

   What about cyber bullying? Do you know what these sites do, if anything, to prevent cyber bullying or inappropriate use of the site?

   Possible answers include these:

   - All sites have terms of use.
   - It is possible to report misuse and abuse of these sites if it is against their rules.
   - They will also remove underage user profiles.

TEACHER TIP
Tweens are nine- to thirteen-year-olds.

7. Display the member code of conduct information for Xanga on transparencies using an overhead projector or on PowerPoint slides using an LCD projector.

8. Explain to the students:

   This is the member code of conduct information from Xanga. Its Web site also has links to report misuse or abuse.

9. Briefly go through the highlighted portions of the code of conduct.

10. Summarize by saying:

    One of the features that the people who created these sites had to consider is how to keep these sites safe, which works sometimes, but not all the time.

11. Explain to the students:

    The people who started these social-networking Web sites had three main things—ideas, ingenuity, and investors. The ideas were theirs, they were smart and clever enough to figure them out, and then they got some big money from investors who saw a way to make even more money through these sites.

    Today we are going to imagine that a company called TechyTeen is interested in investing millions of dollars in a new social-networking Web site that encourages safe and positive interactions among tweens and teens.

    You will be working in your small groups using your ideas and ingenuity—those are your brains and creativity—to come up with a plan for a site like this. You will have today and _____ *(insert date of next session)* **to work on this. Then you will present your plan to the rest of the class. The site**

can have many different features and capabilities—it's up to you. Here is the information from the TechyTeen Company:

12. Read the following fictional notice aloud to the whole class:

    We at the TechyTeen Company are interested in investing a minimum of $25 million dollars to start up a new social-networking Web site for tweens and teens. We envision the Web site to have several different features that promote positive interactions between tweens and teens and the world around them. We see this Web site as being safe and secure for all users. We are open to new ideas and suggestions. Please do not restrict your proposals in any way due to cost. Here are our main guidelines in judging these proposals:

    - **by how strongly they appeal to tweens and teens**
    - **by how safe they are**
    - **by how well they promote positive interactions among teens and their world**

    Thank you very much for your interest,
    The TechyTeen Company

13. Briefly discuss the following questions to get students thinking about the Web site project:

    What are some ways that a Web site could be appealing to both tweens *and* teens?

    Possible answers include the layout, topics, and features.

    What are some ways a Web site could be made safe?

    Possible answers include that people have to sign a form saying they won't do certain things, people have to register with their real contact information to be able to use the site, people have a way to report cyber bullying or illegal behavior, information about cyber bullying is provided on the site, and the site automatically makes profiles private for users under the age of eighteen.

What are some ways that a Web site could promote positive interactions among teens and their world?

Possible answers include features that look for the best instead of the worst, compliment boards, writing stories about positive things people are doing in the world, and creating positive campaigns that raise money for good causes.

14. Divide the class into the peer-led small groups.

15. Explain that the role of the peer leader in these groups is to keep the group on task and to make sure everyone plays a role in getting the project done.

S6-3

16. Hand out a Web Site Planning Packet to each small group.

17. Briefly go through the packet, emphasizing these points:

    - **On the first day** (*or* **today**)**, you will decide the name of your site and what features will be on it. These could be movie reviews, comment pages, profiles, and so on.**

    - **As a group you will brainstorm what these features will be. Then each of you will choose at least one feature to describe in detail using the Facts of the Features sheet.**

    - **You might need to take more time at home to finish these steps.**

    - **During the next session on _____** (*insert date*)**, you will read your Facts of the Features sheets to each other, discuss them, and talk about the look and layout of** the features and the Web site. After that, you will draw the layout of the features and the Web site's home page.

- **You will come up with a policy, or rules, that will keep the site safe and free from cyber bullying.**

- **At the end of the next session, you will decide who will do each part of your class presentation of your social-networking Web site plan on _____** *(insert date)*. **The presentations should be no more than 5 minutes long.**

- **Remember you are trying to impress the TechyTeen Company so it gives your group $25 million to set up this Web site. Keep in mind the three things that are most important to the company—appealing to tweens and teens, safety for users, and positive interactions among tweens and teens throughout the world.**

■ Cyber Bullying

PART 2
30 minutes

▶ **Getting Started**

The purpose of part 2 is for students to work on their social-networking Web site projects.

1. Allow time for students to work on their projects.

2. Circulate among the groups to make sure they are on task and understand the assignment.

PART 3
5 minutes

▶ **Conclusion**

1. Remind students that they need to have the Facts of the Features sheet filled out for the next session on _____ *(insert date)*.

2. Summarize the session by saying that this is their chance to be Web designers and for them to show their creativity in making a plan for a positive Web site for tweens and teens.

Journal Entries

3. Explain:

I will be reading through your conclusions for the journal entries. But I thought you might want to know how things turned out for Allie, J.T., Serena, and Aaron. Your only homework for this session is to read these journal entries so you know what happened.

Hand out the Session 6 Journal Entries.

There is no take-home parent/guardian-student activity for this session.

SESSION 7

Creating a Positive Cyber Site, Part II

Description

Students will fill out a form to commit to helping stop cyber bullying and to explain what they will do if they are aware of cyber bullying situations. Students will also continue to work on their Web site project plans.

Learner Outcomes

By the end of this session, students will be able to

- describe the components of an effective presentation.

- identify how they personally will commit themselves to stop or prevent cyber bullying.

Materials Needed

☐ CD-ROM materials:

- Cyber Solutions sheet S7-1

☐ Materials for the project, including large paper or poster board, markers, and colored pencils

☐ *Optional:* Computers

SESSION 7 AT A GLANCE

Total Time: 50 minutes

Part 1:
Introduction
(5 minutes)

Part 2:
Creating a Positive Cyber Site, Part II
(40 minutes)

Part 3:
Conclusion
(5 minutes)

■ Cyber Bullying

Preparation Needed

1. Print out the Cyber Solutions sheet, one copy per student.

2. Gather project materials.

SESSION 7 OUTLINE

PART 1
5 minutes

▶ **Introduction**

The purpose of part 1 is for students to think about their commitment to stop and/or prevent cyber bullying.

1. Explain to the students:

   We are almost at the end of our unit on cyber bullying, but this won't be the end of our discussions about cyber bullying. In fact, this should just be the beginning of your promise to prevent cyber bullying and help others who are being cyber bullied. I am going to hand out a Cyber Solutions sheet to each of you. You will need to complete the sheet for the next session on _____ *(insert date)* **when you will be giving your presentations.**

   S7-1

2. Hand out the Cyber Solutions sheet now. As time permits, you could allow class time for students to complete the form before the next session.

■ Cyber Bullying

PART 2
40 minutes

▶ **Creating a Positive Cyber Site, Part II**

The purpose of part 2 is for the students to continue to work on the small-group project.

1. Explain to the students that they will now have time to work on their social-networking Web site project.

2. Remind students:

   You should have completed your Facts of the Feature sheets by now. Today you will go over these features in your small groups. Then you will design the layout for these features, as well as the home page for the Web site. You will also need to decide what safety features and policies will be included. By the end of the session, you will also choose who will do each part of your team's presentation on _____
   (*insert date*).

3. Remind students that the TechyTeen Company is willing to spend $25 million on a social-networking Web site that is appealing to tweens and teens, is safe, and promotes positive interactions among teens around the world.

4. Hand out materials, including large pieces of paper, poster boards, markers, and colored pencils, for students to use in their Web site designs.

   Optional: If you have the resources, invite the groups to create their Web site plans on the computer in a PowerPoint presentation.

5. Allow the rest of the class period for students to work on their projects.

PART 3
5 minutes

▶ **Conclusion**

1. Remind students to finish up any work that they have not completed in time for their project presentations on _____ *(insert date)*.

2. Remind students to be thoughtful when they fill out the Cyber Solutions sheet and make a commitment to help stop cyber bullying. Let them know that they will be sharing one of their commitments with the class during the next session.

   There is no take-home parent/guardian-student activity for this session.

SESSION 8

Creating a Positive Cyber Site, Part III

Description

Students will read one of their commitments to the class about how they will stop and/or prevent cyber bullying. They will also present their social-networking Web site project plans to the class.

Learner Outcomes

By the end of this session, students will be able to

- make a public commitment to prevent cyber bullying.
- identify positive ways to use social-networking Web sites.

Materials Needed

☐ CD-ROM materials:

- Web Site Plan Presentation Score Sheet S8-1

☐ *Optional:* Video camera to film the presentations

SESSION 8 AT A GLANCE

Total Time: 50 minutes

Part 1:
Introduction
(10 minutes)

Part 2:
Presenting Your Positive Cyber Sites
(35 minutes)

Part 3:
Conclusion
(5 minutes)

Preparation Needed

1. Print the Web Site Plan Presentation Score Sheet, one copy per student.

2. *Optional:* Make sure the video camera is ready for filming.

3. Mark your calendar for one or two months from today. Set aside some time on that day to give the Cyber Solutions sheets back to the students to look at them again. Have a brief discussion at that time about whether students have acted or have had to act on these commitments. (Caution them not to share names or identifying details in a group setting.)

4. If possible, invite a school administrator to listen to your students' presentations. This person could act as a representative for the TechyTeen Company and pretend to award the $25 million to one group. Or each group could be given an award based on criteria such as these:

    - most appealing to teens
    - safest Web site
    - best at promoting the most positive interactions among teens around the world
    - most creative
    - most organized
    - most original
    - best presentation
    - most user-friendly

SESSION 8 OUTLINE

PART 1
10 minutes

▶ **Introduction**

1. Tell students to take out their Cyber Solutions sheets. They should have these filled out and signed.

2. Go around the room and ask each student to read one of his or her statements aloud to the class so everyone will have heard one commitment from everyone else.

3. Congratulate the students for committing themselves to help prevent cyber bullying.

4. Collect the Cyber Solutions sheets from the students.

5. Explain:

You will look at these sheets again later in the year to discuss whether and how you have acted on these promises.

■ Cyber Bullying

PART 2
35 minutes

▶ **Presenting Your Positive Cyber Sites**

The purpose of part 2 is to have students present their social-networking Web site project plans.

Depending on the number of small groups in your class, student presentations may take another class period to complete.

1. Explain:

   I will call each group to the front to present your project plan to the class. Remember that $25 million dollars is at stake for the best proposal.

S8-1

2. Give each student a Web Site Plan Presentation Score Sheet. Tell the students to fill this out as each group gives its presentation. They will score each group (except their own) based on how well they addressed TechyTeen's criteria of appeal to teens, safety, and positive interactions among teens around the world. The scores will range from 1 to 5 with 1 being the lowest and 5 being the highest. The students will also write on their score sheets one thing they liked about each Web site plan.

3. Remind students that this is not a popularity contest and that you will be grading their score sheets to make sure they were paying attention.

4. Call on each group to give its presentation.

5. Remind the students to speak slowly and loudly so everyone can hear them.

6. Allow a moment for questions or comments after each presentation.

7. After all of the presentations have been given, collect the Web Site Plan Presentation Score Sheets from students.

8. *Option A:* Tally the score sheets for each group and announce a winner at a later date.

   Option B: Reward the (fake) $25 million check to the group that you (or the school administrator attending) think gave the best presentation.

   Option C: Hand out a unique award to each group. Ideas for these unique awards were suggested in this session's Preparation Needed section on page 124.

   Option D: Tell the class that each presentation had something that could be used on the new Web site, so the entire class could work together and win the $25 million.

■ Cyber Bullying

PART 3
5 minutes

▶ **Conclusion**

1. Congratulate the students on their presentations.

2. Summarize by saying:

   You have learned a lot about cyber bullying in the past few weeks. You know how harmful it can be and how to deal with it if it happens to you or someone you know. We'll continue to talk about cyber bullying every once in a while in our class meetings (*or* **in class** *if class meetings aren't held*)**. I hope you'll take seriously the need to stop cyber bullying and all forms of bullying.**

   Stopping cyber bullying begins with everyone making a commitment not to do it, not to spread it or join in, and to report it when it happens. You can begin by using social-networking Web sites and other kinds of technology in a positive way. What you do can make a big difference!

ADDITIONAL MATERIALS
Teacher Training Preparation

Description

This outline includes directions for conducting a 3-hour training for facilitators and teachers of *Cyber Bullying: A Prevention Curriculum for Grades 6–12*. Adapt this outline to fit the needs and timeframe of your group.

Who Should Conduct the Training?

Ideally, several staff and faculty members at the school who help to coordinate the school's bullying prevention activities will conduct the training. For schools that are implementing the *Olweus Bullying Prevention Program (OBPP)*, this training would be led by individuals on the Bullying Prevention Coordinating Committee. If such a committee does not already exist, you may find it beneficial to form one. Members should include an administrator; a teacher from each grade; a school counselor, school psychologist, or other school-based mental-health professional; a representative of the nonteaching staff; one or two parents; and other school personnel (for example, a nurse, school resource officer, Title IX representative), as appropriate.

Materials Needed

- ☐ Copies of the *Cyber Bullying* curriculum, one per person
- ☐ Name tags
- ☐ Marker

■ Cyber Bullying

☐ Pens or pencils

☐ Masking tape

☐ Two pieces of poster board

☐ Your school's policy(ies) on bullying and cyber bullying, if available, as well as its policy on the acceptable use of technology

☐ Game pawns or small slips of paper

☐ CD-ROM materials:

- Peer Leader Packet I-10

- Glossary of Cyber Terms I-11

- Bullying Circle diagram S1-3

- Is It or Isn't It? Peer Leader Instructions, game board, and game cards S2-3, S2-4, S2-5

- Sessions 1–6 Journal Entries S1-1, S2-1, S3-1, S4-1, S5-1, S6-1

- Sessions 1–5 Real-Life Stories S1-2, S2-2, S3-2, S4-2, S5-2, S6-2

- Homework Assignment 3 S3-4 (SP)

- PSA Planning Sheet handout S4-3

- Do First poster and handout I-15, S5-3

- Web Site Planning Packet S6-3

- *Optional:* Computer and LCD projector for the additional background information on cyber bullying that is included as a Teacher Training Presentation on the CD-ROM. I-14

- *Optional:* Refreshments (highly recommended)

Preparation Needed

1. Select a training room in which participants will be comfortable sitting and interacting for 3 hours. Arrange the chairs in a circle or at small tables, so people

will be more open to discussing this sensitive topic with others. Also make sure the room temperature is comfortable.

2. *Optional:* Set up refreshments.

3. Read through this training outline and the curriculum, so you will be comfortable teaching others.

4. Write the Four Anti-Bullying Rules (session 1, page 45) on one sheet of poster board.

5. Create two columns on the second sheet of poster board and write these titles at the top of the columns:

   Traditional bullying is…   Cyber bullying is…

6. Photocopy the Is It or Isn't It? game board, instructions, and game cards to provide one game per group.

7. Highlight statistics from surveys of your own students (for example, from the *Olweus Bullying Questionnaire*) regarding bullying and cyber bullying. If these statistics are not available, research local or state statistics on bullying and/or cyber bullying, or use the statistics shown in the Teacher Training Presentation on the CD-ROM.

 I-14

   Optional: Co-facilitate this training with someone who has a strong background in knowing these statistics.

8. Photocopy all other CD-ROM content to provide one set per person.

Teacher Training Outline

Introduction (30 minutes)

1. Welcome participants and give each person a name tag if they may not all know each other.

2. Introduce yourself and your co-trainer(s) and briefly state why you have chosen to train others in the use of *Cyber Bullying: A Prevention Curriculum for Grades 6–12*.

3. Have people introduce themselves and share briefly why they are interested in learning and teaching this cyber bullying curriculum.

4. Briefly describe the main content of the cyber bullying curriculum by paraphrasing the wording in the Introduction to the Curriculum, pages 1–4.

I-1 to I-16

(SP) S1-1 to S8-1

5. Briefly describe the main components of the curriculum, including the eight sessions, which include the journal entries and real-life stories, the Is It or Isn't It? game, the public service announcements, the Web site project, and the parent/guardian-student homework assignments. Hand out copies of the *Cyber Bullying* curriculum.

6. Highlight and discuss the introductory pages that describe what teachers should be aware of and other guidelines as they teach the curriculum (pages 4–10).

7. Discuss the importance of peer leaders when using this curriculum. Explain how they are chosen and what their

Cyber Bullying

roles will be. (If you are not giving copies of the curriculum to participants, make copies of the Peer Leader Packet, which is the I-10 file on the CD-ROM.)

I-10

Defining Bullying (10 minutes)

1. As a group, discuss or review the definition of bullying (see page 43 in session 1).

2. Display and discuss the Four Anti-Bullying Rules, from the *Olweus Bullying Prevention Program*. If your school is not already following these rules, discuss how they can be implemented in middle and high school classrooms. If your school has already adopted these rules as part of *OBPP*, discuss how they relate to cyber bullying, both on and off campus.

S1-3

3. Distribute and discuss the Bullying Circle diagram and the roles that people play in bullying situations.

4. Briefly share school-level, local, or national statistics on bullying and cyber bullying. Try to personalize this information as much as possible, so participants more clearly see the importance of addressing this issue with their students.

Defining Cyber Bullying (20 minutes)

1. Divide participants into groups of three or four people. Have them brainstorm a list of ways they know of that people can cyber bully.

2. Have each group briefly share a few ideas from its list. Add to the discussion, as necessary.

3. Discuss the differences and similarities between traditional forms of bullying and cyber bullying. Write these ideas on a sheet of poster board that has been prepared following the format in session 2, part 1, starting at step 5 on page 58.

4. Keep participants in their groups. Hand out the Is It or Isn't It? instructions, game board, game cards, and the pawns or slips of paper. If you're using slips of paper, have participants write their names on them and use these in place of game pawns. Allow groups to play the game to give them a better understanding of what cyber bullying is and how students will be using this game.

   S2-3
   S2-4
   S2-5

5. Hand out the Glossary of Cyber Terms and briefly go through the terms and their definitions.

   I-11

The Effects of Cyber Bullying (30 minutes)

1. Share what the warning signs or "red flags" are that someone may be cyber bullying others or being cyber bullied (see Introduction to Cyber Bullying, page 14–15). Stress the importance of teachers' awareness of these warning signs, being proactive in talking with these students to determine what is wrong, and taking action when necessary.

2. *Optional:* Review some of the data from the CD-ROM's Teacher Training Presentation file on possible effects of cyber bullying on students.

   I-14

3. Hand out the Journal Entries and Real-Life Stories. Briefly describe how these are used in each session.

4. Have participants turn to the Session 3 Journal Entries and Session 3 Real-Life Story. Split the participants into five groups of at least two people each, depending on group size. Assign each group a journal entry or the real-life story. They are to read their assigned selection and answer the discussion questions. (If you do not have enough participants to form five groups, create smaller groups or assign more than one selection to one or more groups.) Give the groups 5 minutes to do this. (Allow more time if there are groups assigned to more than one selection.)

   S3-1
   S3-2

5. Invite each group to read its journal entry or story aloud and answer the questions. (Be sure to use the following order when having groups read aloud the entries: Allie, J.T., Serena, Aaron.) After each group finishes, open the floor for discussion. The point of going through this process is to

give participants a better understanding of how cyber bullying can affect tweens and teens and how these activities will be used in classes.

6. Briefly discuss what students will do for the positive text-message language activity and discuss the value of encouraging positive use of text messaging (see pages 76–77).

7. Hand out Homework Assignment 3 so participants have the ABC's of Cyber Bullying Prevention. Discuss any points that may be unclear.

Break (10 minutes)

1. *Optional:* Provide refreshments.

Why People Cyber Bully (10 minutes)

1. Discuss why people cyber bully others (session 4, part 1, starting with step 6, page 84).

SI-3

2. If available, read and discuss your school's policy on cyber bullying. If your school has a policy on bullying that does not specifically mention cyber bullying, discuss how the policy may relate to cyber bullying on (or off) campus. (See the CD-ROM for more information about development of policies on cyber bullying.) If your school does not have a cyber bullying policy, it may have a policy regarding acceptable use of technology that mentions cyber bullying and or other inappropriate uses of campus technology.

Public Service Announcements (PSAs) (20 minutes)

1. Explain the PSA activity from session 4, part 2, to the group (see page 88).

2. Split the participants into groups of three or four people. Hand out a PSA Planning Sheet to each group member. Give groups 10 minutes to brainstorm what they would do for a PSA to stop cyber bullying. Encourage them to write down their ideas.

3. Convene the entire group and invite each small group to share what its PSA would be.

What Can We Do to Stop and Prevent Cyber Bullying? (20 minutes)

1. Distribute the Do First poster and handout.

2. Discuss the handout and how teachers and other school staff can help students feel more comfortable reporting incidents of cyber bullying.

3. Take time to discuss your school's reporting policy of cyber bullying incidents for teachers and other school staff. Be sure to talk about situations when the police should be involved, for example, if the cyber bullying is racially motivated, includes threats to harm, or is defamatory in nature.

I-15
S5-3

Creating a Positive Cyber Site (10 minutes)

1. Take some time to explain this activity from sessions 6–8.

   Introduce the premise for the activity:

   TechyTeen Company is interested in investing $25 million in a new social-networking Web site that encourages safe and positive interactions among tweens and teens.

   Explain the criteria that students will be using to create their plans for their sites:

   - how strongly the sites appeal to tweens and teens
   - how safe they are
   - how well they promote positive interactions among tweens, teens, and their world

   Hand out the Web Site Planning Packet to give participants an idea of how detailed the project should be.

   S6-3

Concluding Activities (20 minutes)

1. If you have a group of school educators, be sure to share with them the Curriculum Scope and Sequence, page 19, and the Related National Academic Standards, page 21.

2. Take time to answer any questions participants may have. Also spend time discussing any special adaptations that may be needed for their specific situations.

3. Finish by having participants discuss and write down several goals for using *Cyber Bullying: A Prevention Curriculum for Grades 6–12*. On a piece of paper, have participants write their basic plan, for example, by answering these questions:

   - When will implementation begin?
   - How often will the curriculum be taught?
   - During what class(es)?
   - How will efforts be evaluated?

   It is important that participants have concrete plans for implementation when they leave your training.

4. Thank everyone for attending. Consider giving participants certificates for their participation in the workshop, or check into whether participants can receive credit toward staff development or professional learning units.

Additional Resources

Recommended Readings

Goodstein, Anastasia. 2007. *Totally wired: What teens and tweens are really doing online.* New York: St. Martin's Griffin.

Kowalski, Robin M., Susan P. Limber, and Patricia W. Agatston. 2008. *Cyber bullying: Bullying in the digital age.* Malden, MA: Blackwell Publishing.

Magid, Larry, and Anne Collier. 2006. *MySpace unraveled: A parent's guide to teen social networking.* Berkeley, CA: Peachpit Press.

Willard, Nancy E. 2007. *Cyberbullying and cyber threats: Responding to the challenge of online aggression, threats, and distress.* New York: Research Press.

Willard, Nancy E. 2007. *Cyber-safe kids, cyber-savvy teens: Helping young people learn to use the Internet safely and responsibly.* New York: Jossey-Bass.

Online Resources

www.hazelden.org/cyberbullying This Web site is specific to this curriculum and also contains information about cyber bullying.

www.cyberbullyhelp.com This Web site includes general information about cyber bullying and information specifically targeted to parents, guardians, and students. Viewers of the site can also read excerpts from the book *Cyber Bullying: Bullying in the Digital Age*.

www.stopbullyingnow.hrsa.gov This interactive Web site sponsored by the U.S. Department of Health and Human Services provides extensive information about bullying, with specific information about cyber bullying.

www.cyberbully.org The Center for Safe and Responsible Internet Use (CSRIU) provides an overview of cyber bullying along with downloadable documents of use to parents, guardians, and educators.

www.cyberbullying.org Along with its companion Canadian site www.cyberbullying.ca, this is one of the original Web sites created to inform individuals about cyber bullying, how to protect oneself against being cyber bullied, and what to do if you are cyber bullied.

www.connectsafely.com An Internet safety site designed for parents, guardians, teens, and experts, this information is designed to facilitate "smart socializing" online and through mobile phones. The site has great tips and information regarding the newest forms of technology.

www.iSafe.org The i-SAFE organization was founded in 1998 to promote safe use of the Internet. From this international leader in Internet safety education, the iSafe.org site provides information for children, parents, guardians, educators, and law-enforcement officials.

www.wiredsafety.org An interactive Web site created by Internet privacy and security lawyer Parry Aftab, this site provides information about cyber bullying and related online abuses.

www.NetSmartz.org Sponsored by the National Center for Missing and Exploited Children, NetSmartz.org is devoted to providing information about Internet safety to children, parents, guardians, educators, and law-enforcement officials.

www.webwisekids.org An interactive Web site for children, parents, guardians, educators, and law-enforcement officials, Web Wise Kids offers interactive programs based on real-world cases to help educate youth about online safety. Online resources and related links are also provided.

www.ikeepsafe.org Governors and their spouses and various law-enforcement agencies founded the Internet Keep Safe Coalition. Its Web site provides information about Internet safety to youth, parents, guardians, and educators.

www.cdc.gov/ncipc/dvp/electronic_aggression.htm This site, maintained by the Centers for Disease Control, provides an overview of cyber bullying, as well as links to several articles published by leading researchers in the field of cyber bullying in a special issue of the *Journal of Adolescent Health*.

www.ed.gov/about/offices/list/os/technology/safety.html This Web site from the U.S. Department of Education offers a listing of Web sites devoted to Internet safety.

www.ncpc.org/topics/by-audience/parents/internet-safety Sponsored by the National Crime Prevention Council, this site provides Internet-safety information tailored to all groups, including youth, parents, guardians, educators, and law-enforcement officials.

www.fbi.gov/publications/pguide/pguidee.htm This Web site provides a downloadable guide for parents and guardians about keeping their children safe from the dangers posed by the Internet. A search of this Web site will show related publications for kids as well.

Video and Digital Resources

Cyberbullying: Cruel Intentions This ABC-sponsored news program focuses on cyber bullying. The program includes a discussion and role-play based on research conducted at Brigham Young University. The program can be ordered online at www.impactpublications.com.

Cyberbullies This program is oriented toward education and prevention. It includes a question-and-answer discussion of cyber bullying and is part of the Taking a Stand: The Bullying Prevention series. The program can be ordered through the Web site www.impactpublications.com.

Adina's Deck This 30-minute film is designed to disseminate information about cyber bullying to nine- to fifteen-year-olds. It has a companion Web site, www.adinasdeck.com, and a teacher's guide.

Ryan's Story and ***What You May Not Know*** When he was thirteen, Ryan Patrick Halligan died by suicide as a result of being cyber bullied. His parents have now created a Web site, www.ryanpatrickhalligan.org, and two DVDs focusing on Internet safety, bullying, specifically cyber bullying, and suicide. Ryan's story includes a companion teacher's guide that allows teachers to discuss why bullying occurs, the effects of bullying on the victim, the role of bystanders, and how to deal with bullying when it does occur. Find more information about these DVDs on Ryan's Web site.

References

Alley, Rebecca, and Susan P. Limber. In press. Legal issues for school personnel. In Susan M. Swearer, Dorothy L. Espelage, Scott A. Napolitano. In press. *Bullying prevention and intervention: Realistic strategies for schools.* New York: Guilford Press.

Arseneault, Louise, Elizabeth Walsh, Kali Trzesniewski, Rhiannon Newcombe, Ashalom Caspi, and Terrie E. Moffitt. 2006. Bullying victimization uniquely contributes to adjustment problems in young children: A nationally representative cohort study. *Pediatrics* 118:130–38.

Eisenberg, Marla E., Dianne Neumark-Sztainer, and Cheryl Perry. 2003. Peer harassment, school connectedness, and academic achievement. *Journal of School Health* 73:311–16.

Fekkes, Minne, Frans I. M. Pijpers, and S. Pauline Verloove-VanHorick. 2004. Bullying behavior and associations with psychosomatic complaints and depression in victims. *Journal of Pediatrics* 144:17–22.

Health Resources and Services Administration. 2008. National Bullying Prevention Campaign. Retrieved from www.stopbullyingnow.hrsa.gov.

International Society for Technology in Education (ISTE). 2007. *National Educational Technology Standards for Students,* 2nd ed. Washington, DC: ISTE.

Joint Committee on National Health Education Standards. 2007. *National Health Education Standards: Achieving Excellence.* 2nd ed. Atlanta: The American Cancer Society.

Juvonen, Jaana, Sandra Graham, and Mark A. Schuster. 2003. Bullying among younger adolescents: The strong, the weak, and the troubled. *Pediatrics* 112:1231–7.

Kowalski, Robin M., and Susan P. Limber. 2007. Electronic bullying among middle school students. *Journal of Adolescent Health* 41:S22–S30.

Kowalski, Robin M., Susan P. Limber, and Patricia W. Agatston. 2008. *Cyber bullying: Bullying in the digital age.* Malden, MA: Blackwell Publishing.

Kowalski, Robin M., Susan P. Limber, Kimball Zane, and Tyler Hassenfeldt. 2008. Cyber bullying: Bullying in the digital age. Paper presented at the annual meeting of the Southeastern Psychological Association, Charlotte, NC.

Lenhart, Amanda. 2007. Cyberbullying and online teens. Retrieved November 15, 2007, from www.pewinternet.org.

Olweus, Dan. 1978. *Aggression in the schools: Bullies and whipping boys.* Hoboken, NJ: John Wiley.

Olweus, Dan. 1993. *Bullying at school: What we know and what we can do.* Malden, MA: Blackwell Publishing.

Olweus, Dan, Susan P. Limber, Vicki Crocker Flerx, Nancy Mullin, Jane Riese, and Marlene Snyder. 2007. *Olweus bullying prevention program: Teacher's guide.* Center City, MN: Hazelden Publishing.

Rigby, Ken. 1997. *Bullying in schools: And what to do about it.* Briston, PA: Jessica Kingsley Publishers.

Rigby, Ken, and Phillip T. Slee. 1993. Dimensions of interpersonal relations among Australian school children and their implications for psychological well-being. *Journal of Social Psychology* 133:33–42.

Willard, Nancy. 2007. Educator's guide to cyberbullying and cyberthreats. Center for Safe and Responsible Internet Use. Retrieved November 15, 2007, from www.cyberbully.org.

About the Authors

Susan P. Limber, Ph.D.

Dr. Susan P. Limber is director of the Center on Youth Participation and Human Rights and professor of psychology at Clemson University. She is a developmental psychologist who received her master's and doctoral degrees in psychology at the University of Nebraska–Lincoln. She also holds a Master's of Legal Studies from Nebraska.

Dr. Limber's research and writing have focused on legal and psychological issues related to youth violence, particularly bullying among children, child protection, and children's rights. She directed the first wide-scale implementation and evaluation of the *Olweus Bullying Prevention Program* in the United States and co-authored the *Blueprint for the Bullying Prevention Program*, as well as many other articles on the topic of bullying. In recent years, she has directed the training for the *Olweus Bullying Prevention Program* in the United States. She has provided consultation to the National Bullying Prevention Campaign, supported by the Health Resources and Services Administration.

In 1997, she received the Saleem Shah Award for early career excellence in psychology–law policy, awarded by the American Psychology–Law Society of the American Psychological Association (Division 41) and the American Academy of Forensic Psychiatry. In 2004, Dr. Limber received the American Psychological Association's Early Career Award for Psychology in the Public Interest.

Robin M. Kowalski, Ph.D.

Dr. Robin M. Kowalski is a professor of psychology at Clemson University. She obtained her doctoral degree in social psychology from the University of North Carolina at Greensboro. Her research interests focus primarily on aversive interpersonal behaviors, most notably complaining, teasing, and bullying, with a particular focus on cyber bullying. She is the author or co-author of several books, including *Complaining, Teasing, and Other Annoying Behaviors*; *Social Anxiety*; *Aversive Interpersonal Behaviors; Behaving Badly; The Social Psychology of Emotional and Behavioral Problems;* and *Cyber Bullying: Bullying in the Digital Age*. Her research on complaining brought her international attention, including an appearance on NBC's *Today Show*.

Dr. Kowalski has received several awards, including Clemson University's Award of Distinction, Clemson University's College of Business and Behavioral Science Award for Excellence in Undergraduate Teaching, the Phil Prince Award for Excellence and Innovation in Teaching, and the Clemson Board of Trustees Award for Faculty Excellence.

Patricia W. Agatston, Ph.D.

Dr. Patricia W. Agatston is co-author of the book *Cyber Bullying: Bullying in the Digital Age* with Robin M. Kowalski, Ph.D., and Susan P. Limber, Ph.D., recently published by Blackwell Publishers. She is also a nationally certified trainer and technical assistance consultant for the *Olweus Bullying Prevention Program*. She has been quoted in articles on cyber bullying in *Time Magazine* and *Good Housekeeping* magazine and has appeared on *Mom Talk Radio* and *Mornings* with Lorri Allen and Larry Estepa on FamilyNet Television. She was a participant in the CDC's expert panel on Electronic Media and Youth Violence and has presented nationally and internationally on cyber bullying.

Dr. Agatston is a licensed professional counselor (LPC) with the Cobb County School District's Prevention/Intervention Center in Marietta, Georgia. A founding board member for SafePath Children's Advocacy Center in Marietta, Georgia, Dr. Agatston received the Coalition for Child Abuse Prevention's VIP Award in 2005.

Hazelden, a national nonprofit organization founded in 1949, helps people reclaim their lives from the disease of addiction. Built on decades of knowledge and experience, Hazelden offers a comprehensive approach to addiction that addresses the full range of patient, family, and professional needs, including treatment and continuing care for youth and adults, research, higher learning, public education and advocacy, and publishing.

A life of recovery is lived "one day at a time." Hazelden publications, both educational and inspirational, support and strengthen lifelong recovery. In 1954, Hazelden published *Twenty-Four Hours a Day*, the first daily meditation book for recovering alcoholics, and Hazelden continues to publish works to inspire and guide individuals in treatment and recovery, and their loved ones. Professionals who work to prevent and treat addiction also turn to Hazelden for evidence-based curricula, informational materials, and videos for use in schools, treatment programs, and correctional programs.

Through published works, Hazelden extends the reach of hope, encouragement, help, and support to individuals, families, and communities affected by addiction and related issues.

For questions about Hazelden publications, please call **800-328-9000** or visit us online at **hazelden.org/bookstore**.